COMMEDIA OZ

Playing Commedia in Contemporary Australia

Steven Gration and Nicky Peelgrane

includes STARDUST,
an Australian Commedia script
by Steven Gration

First published in 2008 by
Currency Press Pty Ltd
PO Box 2287
Strawberry Hills NSW 2012 Australia
www.currency.com.au
enquiries@currency.com.au

National Library of Australia Cataloguing-in-Publication Data:

Author:	Gration, Steven
Title:	Commedia Oz : playing commedia in contemporary Australia / authors, Steven Gration; Nicky Peelgrane.
Publisher:	Strawberry Hills, N.S.W. : Currency Press, 2008.
ISBN:	9780868198200 (pbk.)
Notes:	Includes index.
	Bibliography.
Subjects:	Lecoq, Jacques--Interviews.
	Commedia dell'arte.
	Commedia dell'arte--Handbooks, manuals, etc.
	Commedia dell'arte--History.
	Acting--Handbooks, manuals, etc.
	Actors--Australia.
	Theatrical producers and directors--Australia.
	Comedy.
Other Authors/Contributors:	Peelgrane, Nicky.
Dewey Number:	792.23

Cover design by Kate Florance / Laura McLean
Typeset in Adobe Garamond Pro
Printed by Ligare Book Printers, Riverwood NSW

Steven Gration is a director, writer, actor, puppeteer and teacher. He has taught Drama, Acting and Media Studies in post-primary, indigenous and tertiary institutions in Victoria, South Australia, Queensland and the Northern Territory. He has been a guest artist in Mexico, Malaysia, Singapore, Japan, France, England and the USA. Steven has a Bachelor of Education (Drama/Media Studies) University of Melbourne (MSC) and is currently conducting PhD research into *The Praxis of the Solo Performer* at Griffith University, Queensland, where he is an affiliate member of the Centre for Public Culture and Ideas. He has worked professionally as a performer and/or director with theatre companies including Handspan, The Woolly Jumpers, Corrugated Iron Youth Theatre, Magpie Theatre (State Theatre Company of South Australia), Queensland Theatre Company and Kite Theatre. He has written several plays which have been professionally produced including his children's play *Chutney*, which was published in 2001 by Playlab Press.

Steven was nominated for a Victorian Green Room Director's Award for his production of Roger Bennett's *Funerals and Circuses*, with music by Paul Kelly. This play had sell-out seasons at the 1992 Adelaide Festival of Arts, the 1993 Melbourne International Festival of Arts and the 1993 National Festival of Theatre, Canberra.

Nicky Peelgrane is a teaching artist, actor, director and producer of Drama for and by young people. Nicky holds a Bachelor of Arts and a Graduate Diploma in Secondary Education (Drama and English). Since beginning teaching in 1997, she has worked with students from Early Education Units and Years 1 to 12, as well as Continuing Education Drama for adult students. Nicky has worked with students from Middlemount (Queensland) to Muswellbrook (NSW) and many places in between. She has produced and directed countless performances, working with students to help them artistically articulate the issues they believe to be important.

Both Steven and Nicky have contributed to the writing of this book. Many of their experiences were shared when Nicky was cast in Steven's play, *Stardust*, in 2000, which toured schools in Brisbane, the Gold Coast and Sunshine Coast. Nicky and Steven have drawn upon their personal experiences and professional practice in their determination to assist students, teachers and performers in the study and playing of Commedia in an Australian context.

The illustrator, **Benjamin Drake**, was born in 1987 and raised in the pine forests of Queensland's Sunshine Coast hinterland by a pair of wild artists. These artists, wishing their children to have a good income later in life, made them promise never to go to art college. Although Benjamin devoted his studies to sciences in high school, his arty ways got the better of him and upon his graduation in 2004 he enrolled in the Bachelor of Animation course at Queensland College of Art, where he is currently studying and living in Brisbane.

FOREWORD

Many years ago Steve Gration asked me to write a play that used the characters from Commedia dell'arte. I wish I'd had this book to help me, even if only for the spelling. How Steve and his cast made any sense of 'Aelekena', 'Punchetere', 'Bingadonnolo' and their adventures is beyond me.

I remember turning up to a workshop and sitting there dumbfounded as the actors sat around in masks looking into pretend mirrors and making weird animal noises. I seem to recall the next workshop featured the actors, Steve, some girls from the office and myself writhing around on the ground pretending to wear masks and making weird animal noises. The last workshop was cancelled. 'Well, that's it,' said Steve, 'now go off and write the play. You've got a week.' I went home and stared at the blank screen of my Amstrad word processor for an hour or so and then started to type up what I now realise was a piece of rubbish. Steve was polite enough to accept my work, honourable enough to pay me and desperate enough to put it on. It toured the schools and offended many. Hopefully there were a few laughs.

My lasting image is of Francis Greenslade, playing (I think) Dottore and hobbling around the stage with a bicycle lashed to his leg. I know I laughed a lot but I wonder if anyone else did.

I commend and recommend Steve Gration and Nicky Peegrane's book to you. Comedy is a wondrous W. Heath Robinson-type machine capable of being re-tooled in many ways to produce a myriad of gags. You need a sense of humour to run it and this book is a most helpful Instruction Manual.

Shaun Micallef
October 2007

CONTENTS

ACKNOWLEDGEMENTS

Steven Gration: I wish to thank my drama teachers at Maribyrnong High School between 1967–72, Joan Brogden and Ray Kenny; David Lander, an innovative and highly skilled improvisation and mask teacher and my colleagues in his company, Mad Hat Theatre (1974–6); my fellow actors at The Woolly Jumpers Theatre for Schools, Geelong (1984–7); Melbourne-based actor Paolo Bongiovanni; the 1989–90 members of Corrugated Iron Youth Theatre, Darwin; the late Jacques Lecoq for his generosity in agreeing to an interview during his only Australian visit in 1991; the 1991–3 acting ensembles—especially Fille Dusseljee, Francis Greenslade, Nicholas Hope, Kate Roberts, Mandy Sandilands and *Prince of Numbskulls* playwright Shaun Micallef—during my time as Artistic Director of Magpie Theatre, South Australia; Dominique Sweeney and Michael Newbold, two creative and inspirational Commedia teachers, performers and devisors; Wayne Anthoney, clown extraordinaire; the students and staff of Theatre Studies at Griffith University, Gold Coast (1995–2005); Queensland-born actor and playwright Adam Grossetti; and finally Nicky Peelgrane for her patience and persistence in the development of this book. *Commedia Oz* has emerged as a result of creative work and experiments conducted with these artists and their observations of an extensive menu of characters living in Australia.

Nicky Peelgrane: I wish to thank many people who contributed to this book. Since teachers are bowerbirds and tend to collect bits and pieces from everywhere, there are many activities and ideas that I absorbed from my career in teaching. Now that I try to remember where they came from, it is all a big, messy, blue nest—humble apologies if there is anyone missed. Thanks in particular go to my first drama teacher Kate Holt; Sue Lawson for her inspiration and support during my practicum placement at Kenmore SHS; Brendan Glanville of the Australian Acting Academy, as well as staff members Kim and Seb; and the collegiate support of Drama Queensland. For inspiration, encouragement and kindness, thank you to some wonderful people from QUT: Judith McLean, Brad Haseman, Christine Comans, Sandra Gattenhof and Julie Dunn (now at Griffith University). For fantastic feedback, thank you to Jo Wise. For help with the 'Bog In!' section, thank you to Sean Lubbers. Most importantly, I wish to acknowledge the contribution of the thousands of students I have worked with over the years. They are the enthusiastic guinea pigs who have helped shape, refine and define the activities discussed herein. They have prompted me to consolidate my teaching skills over the years; they have kept me inspired, constantly laughing and in love with my profession. Thank you also to Steven Gration for being such an inspiring director and believing that this book was possible. Much appreciation goes to the friends and family (you know who you are) who helped with child care. Finally, I wish to thank my husband Simon Finnigan, without whom I would never have had the courage to do any of this, phenomenologically speaking of course!

We both wish to thank Michael Sams, Mary Eggleston and Kurt Duvall for their wonderful ideas and enthusiasm and their unique character interpretations in the 2000 production of *Stardust*. Thank you also to Jo Thomas of Commotion! for her assistance in producing *Stardust*. Jointly, we wish to thank Ian Brown and Don Batchelor for their helpful feedback and assistance with this text and Ben Drake for his inspiring *Commedia Oz* illustrations. We are grateful to Lucas Dawson for his photographs of Steven's Commedia masks—the Arlecchino mask was made by Meghann Montgomery and the Neutral Mask by Russell Fewster. The Brighella mask was designed by Fille Dusseljee and made by Peter Donahue. All other masks were designed by Sylvia Rech and made by Peter Donahue. All masks in photographs except the Tartaglia mask and the Neutral Mask were used in the performance of *Stardust*. Finally, we both wish to thank Victoria Chance and the people at Currency Press.

INTRODUCTION: How to Navigate this Book

Commedia Oz is an Australian apprentice theatre-makers' training manual for teachers, students, actors and directors who want to learn about the comic performance form known as Commedia dell'arte. Arguably, the two greatest things to have come out of Italy are the Commedia tradition and Spaghetti Bolognese! Throughout this book we have created an analogy between a Commedia student's progress and a chef's apprenticeship in Italian food. As with the humble Aussie version of 'spag bol', Commedia has, in turn, been given a unique Aussie flavour by the people who make and shape Drama. Some of our recipes have been prepared earlier, others are to be improvised in your kitchen.

STRUCTURE

This book examines Commedia's early beginnings and traditions, then offers exercises and experiences that will shape the Commedia apprentice. You will also find a professional script that has been successfully used by actors, suggestions to teachers for assessment, and finally a glossary of terms.

STARDUST, A CONTEMPORARY AUSTRALIAN COMMEDIA PLAY

In 2000, Steven wrote *Stardust,* a script for performance in Queensland schools, specifically for Drama students. The full script is to be found in Chapter 7 and is an Australian interpretation of the traditional Commedia recipe.

We recommend teachers and students—our apprentice Commedia chefs—read through *Stardust* before commencing the theoretical reading and practical exercises in the early Chapters of the book which contain many references to the script. Then, when you revisit *Stardust* after the training exercises, as experienced apprentices you will be in a position to offer new tastes and original recipes of your own when performing scenes from the script. You may even wish to open your own restaurant by staging an entire production of *Stardust.*

The character costume illustrations in this book are contemporary and an example of one way of modernising the Commedia tradition. Photographs in Chapter 2 are of masks worn during rehearsal and performance in the original *Stardust* production.

What's in the italics?

At the end of each section, you will find Response Questions which refer back to both the Chapter and the practical experiences of the students. These questions:

- *could be springboards for discussion to assist the flow of the lesson, and/or*
- *could be assigned to students or used as a guide for students in keeping a responding journal of their experiences, and/or*
- *could also be used as frameworks for assessment tasks.*

What's between the lines?

During the production and performance period of **Stardust** in 2000, both Steven Gration and Nicky Peelgrane kept Journals of their experiences. Steven kept a Director's Journal and Nicky an Actor's Journal. It is interesting that, despite the wealth of information on the history of Commedia in Italy and beyond, very little has been written from either a Director's or an Actor's point of view. Past literature reveals only glimpses of what it was like to perform or devise Commedia. We hope that excerpts from our Journals will enhance your understanding of Commedia dell'arte and how professional theatre troupes work. We also hope that our experiences will provide you with useful ingredients to enrich the recipes you create in your own performances.

CHAPTER 1

Setting the Table: Foundations and Strong Influences

BASIC ITALIAN STOCK

In order to understand Commedia dell'arte (pronounced *com-med-ee-ya dell art-ay*) in a contemporary Australian context, the apprentice must firstly explore the Commedia's historical foundations.

The Commedia dell'arte seems to have emerged as a popular form of entertainment in Italy around 1545 and was at its height from the 1560s until it began to fade in the mid-1700s. The term 'Commedia dell'arte' was coined in the eighteenth century and means 'Comedy of Skill' or 'Professional Comedy'. It was a comedy practised by professional artists in the tradition of other medieval craft guilds such as goldsmiths, blacksmiths and shipwrights.

In essence, Commedia was stylised acting by professional performers who used stock characters (*tippi fissi*) and improvised around basic scenarios (*canovacci*). The humour was both physical (*lazzi*) and verbal (*burle*). Commedia troupes usually consisted of ensembles of between eight and twelve actors, a number of musicians, assistants, stagehands and a manager-director. They would perform on outdoor, raised, portable stages with simple painted backdrops in town squares and marketplaces. These stages were quite small in size, typically five metres wide and three metres deep. However, when a troupe was in favour with royalty and the nobility, it could find itself performing in large halls and ballrooms in palaces and mansions.

After many years of studying and teaching Commedia dell'arte to his students in Paris, the brilliant theatre pedagogue and director, Jacques Lecoq, developed the term *la comédie humaine* ('the human comedy') to describe the nature of Commedia. In this *comédie*, 'The limits of human nature emerge… bringing to the surface the tragedy that lies buried beneath it…' He goes on to say, 'All the characters are frightened… of being tricked, of starving, of dying, etc…' (Lecoq:

2001) It would seem that the concerns of the characters of the human comedy of the sixteenth century are not that different to the fundamental ones we face in our current époque.

FILM, RADIO, TELEVISION AND THEATRE

The twentieth century saw a widespread revival of interest in the Commedia dell'arte as it slipped seamlessly into film and television comedy. Its influence can be easily recognised every time Kramer bursts into Jerry Seinfeld's apartment (*lazzi*); or when Jerry breaks the story to tell a joke in a stand-up comedy segment (*burle*). When the loveable but gentle Kenny in the Australian film of the same name fills the arrogant corporate executive's car with sewage after blocking in Kenny's truck; when Mr Burns from the animated series 'The Simpsons' jealously guards his wealth and privacy; when Australian performer Barry Humphries masquerades as Dame Edna Everage or Sir Les Patterson; every time a stand-up comedian plies their stock-in-trade or a street busker attracts a passing audience before performing a special trick—all owe a debt to the Commedia dell'arte. Even on the television 'Football Shows' (NRL or AFL) when the host dresses in disguise (sometimes as a woman) to satirise a well-known commercial, television program or celebrity, Commedia is not far away.

Other examples abound. Guests like Shaun Micallef rely on wit and intuition when thrown into an unfamiliar role or situation in Australian television's 'Thank God You're Here'; a Theatresports player improvises within a game structure; actor Jim Carrey throws himself physically into his characters in the films *Dumb and Dumber, The Mask* and *Liar Liar*; a circus clown slips and tumbles acknowledging the delight of the audience; in the television program 'Fawlty Towers', when Basil Fawlty slaps the servant, Manuel, over the back of the head—these performers have all been inspired by the Commedia dell'arte tradition.

The list of examples goes on. Monty Python's 'Ministry for Silly Walks'; the Looney Tunes cartoon character's Wile E. Coyote's futile chase of the Road Runner; the slapstick violence of television's veteran Three Stooges with its strict henpecking order (Mo is number one, followed by Larry, with Curly at the bottom of the pile); the Marx Brothers singing and dancing to distract the antagonists; the silly voices and absurd predicaments of the 1950s radio classic series 'The Goon Show'; the evolution of Australian entertainers Mo (Roy Rene), George Wallace and Gladys Moncrieff from vaudeville to live radio and Graham 'The King' Kennedy from radio to television; the teaming-up of opposite personalities such as Bob Hope and Bing Crosby, Abbott and Costello (not the Australian politicians!), Laurel and Hardy—all would be right at home in a Commedia dell'arte troupe.

In 1947, Piccolo Teatro company in the Italian city of Milan performed Goldoni's famous Commedia play *A Servant of Two Masters* (1743), the company's members having rediscovered the art of making leather masks and the demanding skills of improvisation and physical performance. Piccolo's director, Giorgio Strehler, combined forces with Paolo Grassi, Dario Fo, Jacques Lecoq, Etienne Decroux and Amleto Sartori to inspire and influence European theatre and future generations of performers into the twenty-first century. Early in the twentieth century, Soviet theatre director and actor Vsevolod Meyerhold (1874–1942) and the Frenchman Jacques Copeau (1879–1949) injected the spirit of the Commedia into their actor training and into performances for their audiences.

VISUAL ART

In Spain in the early 1900s, Pablo Picasso captured the essence of Commedia characters in his early sketches, drawings and paintings. Picasso's unique style helped reignite public interest in Commedia.

SILENT FILM

When the silent film star Charlie Chaplin (the Little Hobo) wins out over the bad guys through his naiveté and physical prowess; when Buster Keaton stands emotionless and unharmed as a building collapses over the top of him; when Harold Lloyd hangs perilously from the hands of London's Big Ben clock; and every time Mack Sennett's Keystone Cops pile into one another after a wild chase—all have honoured the basic elements of a Commedia performance.

A SCHOOLBOY PRANK—TOWARDS ABSURD THEATRE

In France during 1888, a schoolboy, Alfred Jarry, created a grotesque Commedia-like puppet character, Père Ubu, to satirise one of his teachers. In so doing, he inspired the Surrealist and Dada movements and a performance genre referred to sixty years later as Theatre of the Absurd. Writers such as Ionesco, Beckett and Pirandello owe much to Jarry and his reminder of the excesses of human greed with his Ubu plays, most notably *Ubu Roi*, and human frailty with Jarry's own death through alcoholism in 1907, pointing to the tragic underbelly of Commedia dell'arte.

LITERATURE

The dark side of obsessive love and the intervention of a hunchback bell-ringing servant in Victor Hugo's 1830s French novel, *The Hunchback of Notre Dame* and the earlier work of Spanish writer Miguel de Cervantes Saavedra in 1605 with *Don Quixote de la Mancha,* featuring the servant Sancho Panza, both draw from the wide menu of characters offered by travelling Commedia troupes.

ELIZABETHAN AND ROYAL COURT THEATRE

Numerous characters, storylines and themes in the plays of the Spanish writer, Lope de Vega, and the French master of theatre, Molière, including his version of the zany servant Scapin and romantic portrayals of Harlequin and Columbine; many of the plots and characters of Shakespeare including *The Merchant of Venice* and *Romeo and Juliet*; the cursing and carrying-on of the gate keeper in *Macbeth* and the gravediggers in *Hamlet*; Britain's fascination with Punch (Pulcinella) in the Punch and Judy puppet shows—all are testimony to the power, skill and entertainment of the travelling Commedia troupes of the past. Every element of Western performance culture which makes us laugh has almost certainly been borrowed or adapted consciously or unconsciously from the sixteenth-century Italian Comedy, the Commedia dell'arte.

COMMEDIA DELL'ARTE CONVENTIONS

What is it that distinguishes the Commedia dell'arte from other performance styles? While some genres of theatre *may* contain a couple of the following elements, only Commedia uniquely combines *all* of these conventions which are discussed in more detail following this summary:

- Actors wore half or three-quarter leather masks to portray stock characters complemented by readily identifiable costumes.
- The stock or archetypal characters were drawn from specific regions, personality types and social classes.
- Improvisation took priority over 'sticking to a script'. The actors had a licence to play with basic sequences, storylines and scenario outlines (*canovacci*).
- Women were (eventually) permitted to perform in the Commedia while in most of Europe, Britain and Asia they were, at the time, banned from performing.
- Slapstick violence and high physicality, including stock gestures, acrobatics, dance and clowning were utilised.

- Sexual pranks, innuendo and crudeness were rife.
- Physical (*lazzi*) and verbal (*burle*) gags and jokes interrupted the plot purely for audience entertainment.
- *Grummelot*, or spoken gibberish, allowed the actor to communicate to audiences by transcending language differences.
- The troupes used political and social commentary, criticising or making fun of international, national and local personalities, and referring to events and news of the day.

These conventions were undoubtedly utilised to engage and entertain audiences in open-air marketplaces and village squares. However, organisers needed to be mindful that a show could be cancelled on a whim by kings, nobles and the wealthy if a performance didn't take their fancy or, even worse, gave offence.

As we look at these nine major conventions in more depth, we discover that the professional performers involved in Commedia troupes were acute observers of the world in which they lived.

1. Masks

The Commedia masks were half or three-quarter masks to ensure the actor's jaw and mouth were free to speak and project outdoors and in large venues. In cultures which use full masks it is unusual for an actor wearing a mask to speak as the voice becomes trapped behind the mask. A specific opening or mouthpiece would need to be built into the design (as with some Ancient Greek Chorus masks) or an articulated jaw piece (in some Asian masks). Commedia masks were made of leather to mould to the wearer's face and to allow the actor's skin to breathe through the material. Leather also kept the textural relationship between an actor's skin and the mask much closer than fabric or wooden masks may have done.

Masks and costumes quickly identified the characters and their origins and gave the actors wearing them a spontaneity and power that non-mask actors of the period could not generate. The mask of the foolish, playful servant Arlecchino contained cat and/or monkey-like qualities and had a large visible bump on one side of the forehead. It has been argued that this was the remnant of a devil's horn that signified his mischievous behaviour. Alternatively, the mark may have indicated that he came from Bergamo where the people were farmers and often outdoors in the hot sun tending their olive groves and therefore accumulating many moles, freckles and sunspots. The distinct green, black and red diamond shapes on his white costume, combined with his distinctive mask, made Arlecchino instantly recognisable to audiences even before he spoke. Today's audiences probably have the same relationship with their favourite characters from television shows such as 'Home and Away', 'Kath and Kim', 'Friends', 'Seinfeld' and 'Neighbours'.

2. Stock Characters

Regional dialects and accents were often spoken by the characters according to their origins. The accents of Arlecchino and Brighella were from Bergamo, Pantalone from Venice, Pulcinella from Naples, Il Dottore from the academic world of the University of Bologna, and the Captain was often played with a heavy Spanish accent. In various parts of Italy many audience members could not understand dialects or accents that differed from their own. When the troupes toured France, Spain and Germany the audience could hardly understand a word, but such was the physical skill of the actors that they developed a gestural and physical language which they combined with *grummelot* (gibberish), so that non-speakers in the audience could easily follow the performance.

The stock characters could generally be divided into four families:

- **THE MASTERS** These include Il Dottore and Pantalone and sometimes Tartaglia as a low-ranking master (all masked). A masked character called Il Magnifico made a rare appearance in some troupes but was less foolish than Il Dottore and Pantalone.
- **THE SERVANTS** *Zanni*, including Arlecchino, Brighella, Pulcinella (all masked), Columbina (unmasked) and sometimes Tartaglia as a high-ranking servant.
- **THE LOVERS** These include females (*inamorata*), such as Isabella and Fiorinetta, and males (*inamorato*), such as Flavio, Lelio and Sylvio (all unmasked).
- **THE MILITARY** Often foreigners such as Il Capitano (masked).

Servant characters were referred to by the generic name, *zanni*. The term probably originates from the fact that the above-mentioned characters were the 'descendants of the *sonnio* (Latin) characters of the ancient Roman *Atellanae* [fables]'. (Duchartre: 1966) Another explanation for the term is based on one of the oldest troupes touring Europe 'who were managed by Zan Ganassa and thereafter *Zan* or *Zanni* was used as a prefix to proper servants' names'. (Erenstein: 1990) Yet another explanation is that *Zan(ni)* is nothing more than a diminutive in the Lombard dialect for the Christian name Giovanni (Little John or Johnny).

But whatever the origins, *zanni* is now a common term for all and any of the comic servants in the Commedia dell'arte. (And the word 'zany' is often used nowadays to describe eccentric and humorous people.) Of the servants, Arlecchino and Brighella became the most loved and well known. When it came to raw sexual desire, farts, enemas, phalluses, gorging on food, verbal and physical sexual innuendo, the *zanni* were the driving force, followed closely by Pantalone and Il Capitano.

The Lovers remained mostly innocent and above all the base humour, although they too, on occasion, could 'make their appearance in the most scanty attire and enjoy the freest sort of adventures'. (Duchartre: 1966)

See Chapter 2 for details on characters' personalities, obsessions, masks, costumes and behaviour.

3. Improvisation

Combining the power of the mask and a licence to improvise would ensure that no two Commedia performances would ever be exactly the same even if based on the same plot with the same characters. Often the plots revolved around simple stories, such the poor boy and the rich girl next door falling in love. The father of the girl is arranging her marriage to a rich, older man or, perhaps, the Captain. The girl enlists the help of her servants to elope with her true love. After scenes of disguise, theft, chase, slapstick fights and so on, true love wins through.

Alternatively, a storyline might explore the greed of the servants and their attempts to steal from their wealthy employer. They are, of course, discovered but forgiven when their foolishness inadvertently reveals the Captain to be a coward, a liar and with dishonourable intentions towards the master's beautiful daughter who then marries her true love, the boy next door.

Before each performance a list of scenes in the order in which they were to be played (*canovacci*) would be placed backstage. *Canovaccio* (the singular form) literally means 'that which is on the canvas'. Its description could be as simple as:

> *Pantalone sends Arlecchino on an errand to deliver an important letter to Il Dottore. Pantalone has trouble making the task clear to Arlecchino.*

The actors playing these two roles would improvise around the scenario using some set dialogue and gesture, but with much improvised slapstick, insults, verbal and physical gags. They would try to gauge how much the audience was enjoying the scene before they ended it and moved onto the next scene on the *canovacci*. The improvisation also allowed for the characters to interact directly with the audience, fielding verbal responses and perhaps throwing comments back in much the same way as stand-up comedians do today.

Arlecchino (left) and Columbina (right) in *Stardust*

Illustrations by Benjamin Drake

> It is true that serious actors, and especially actresses, in this kind of comedy possess an extraordinary store of varied material which they exploit at will for pleas, reproaches, and moods of despair and jealousy. Yet, knowing this, it is nonetheless astonishing to see them improvising before the public and to observe how appropriately they select their material, always having the right quips ready and expressing them with such energy that they wring applause from the audience.
>
> (*Memoires*, Carlo Gozzi cited in Duchartre: 1966)

4. Women

Although they didn't appear in performances until perhaps the late 1560s, nearly all the women of the Commedia could dance, sing and play the guitar or other stringed instruments and many could speak several languages. The beautiful Isabella Andreini, who belonged to Flaminio Scala's famous I (Comici) Gelosi Troupe (1572–1604), was a member of several academic institutions and a distinguished Latin scholar. She married the actor Francesco Andreini, who at that time took over the directing of I Gelosi. Isabella's beauty, intelligence and cultivation were the talk and admiration of France and Italy even though she was only sixteen years old. The role of the *inamorata* (female lover) became associated with her portrayal of it and thus 'Isabella' eventually became the name of the character. She was also a talented poet and composed music, sonnets and songs.

The custom of giving women a share in performance apparently had its origins in the Dorian countries during the time of the Roman Empire. Here, for the first time, the female lover was the most important character, and the concept of the leading lady passed over into Sicily, and then Rome. The Commedia troupes must have drawn on this knowledge of women performing in ancient times, but in France and England young men enacted women's parts until the 1760s.

5. Physicality

Slapstick, mime and stock gestures were important elements in the physical language of the Commedia, transcending the barriers of the spoken word, particularly when touring France, Germany, Spain and England. For example, to display his desire for money, Pantalone might constantly rub his hands together. A character expressing fear or surprise might throw both arms up as if in surrender.

> When the first Italian companies came to France they played in their native tongue, but they had of necessity inherited the traditions of their art to such a degree that they were able to make their Parisian audiences understand them without difficulty by virtue of their clever mimicry.
>
> (Duchartre: 1966)

Perhaps the closest we have to this physical language is the comedy and melodrama of the silent film era. The term 'slapstick' almost certainly derives from a bat used by Pulcinella and Arlecchino that made a loud 'clap' when struck on another character's behind—literally a 'slap stick'. This instrument, constructed of two small lengths of timber separated by a wooden block near the handle, probably has its origins in the ancient comic characters of the Romans or as far back as the classical Greeks. These days, any physical comic routines which include slipping over a banana peel, doors slamming in faces, chases, collisions, pie throwing, routines with planks and ladders, etc. are considered 'slapstick comedy'.

Rowan Atkinson's Mr Bean is a good contemporary example of a slapstick character, relying on physical and gestural language to communicate rather than words. In fact, one of the key principles of Commedia performance is to avoid unnecessary talking on stage. In other words (no pun intended), if an actor can communicate the idea, relationship, status, mood, character trait or plot point through physicality rather than the spoken word, or to complement the spoken word, then the actor should exploit the physical.

6. Innuendo

The heartbeat of the Commedia was the antics of the servants. Much of the slapstick comedy and violence was initiated by them or imposed upon them. The same could be said for the sexual pranks, innuendo and the less tasteful antics on stage. These might manifest as the Dottore chasing a servant with a giant enema device; or the Captain, upon spying Isabella, might say to her, 'I notice your bud is blossoming, you beautiful rose. I'd like to pluck your petals.'

With such activities and goings-on, the Commedia troupes could find themselves in and out of favour with royalty, the Church and civil authorities. When in favour they were as highly paid and sought after as today's pop stars. When out of favour they had to scurry out of town for fear of their lives!

7. *Lazzi* and *Burle*

Lazzi (plural) has a multiplicity of meanings, but generally refers to physical comic routines that can be either planned or spontaneous. A *lazzo* (singular) does not necessarily advance the plot or make a contribution to the progress of the action, yet it is often one of the funniest moments for an audience. The term *'lazzo'* means 'turn', 'trick' or 'Italian business'. A *lazzo* can be physical and acrobatic with a light touch; or it can be longer and end with a verbal gag or joke, often referred to as *burle*. The word *lazzi* may also mean 'knots' deriving from the Tuscan word *'lacci'*. (Duchartre: 1966) Other related terms include the Roman *'trionfi'* (triumphs) and *'azzi'* (actions) or the French *'jeu'* (play).

A *lazzo* could be used when a popular character was playing in a region from which they originated—Pulcinella in Naples, Arlecchino and Brighella in

Bergamo—or because on a particular day the audience warmed to a specific character. The *lazzo* could also cover for a time-consuming costume change such as the *inamorata* changing into a ball gown or wedding dress. It could also be used to cover for someone who was injured and being attended to backstage or if an actor missed their entry, missed a cue or dropped lines. It often occurred spontaneously as a result of some extraneous stimuli or simply arose from the imagination of an inspirational actor. The following is an example:

> It is a hot summer's day outdoors in the marketplace and the actor playing Arlecchino has a troublesome fly swooping on him. The actor decides to chase the fly, justifying this behaviour by saying he is very hungry (always one of the main complaints of this character). He does amazing tumbles and acrobatics to catch the fly, and when he succeeds, much to the audience's disgust, he swallows it. But as he ingests the fly, it remains alive inside his body causing him to conduct even more amazing and contorted acrobatics depending on which part of his internals or limbs the fly moves to, until the fly eventually dies or Arlecchino flies off in a comic exit.

Other examples of *lazzi* and *burle* appear in Chapter 5 and Chapter 7 (*Stardust*).

Often audiences were a long distance from the stage, going about their business in a busy marketplace, therefore *lazzi* and *burle* were used as a way of luring people over to watch the spectacle. Tickets were not purchased as we do in the theatre today. Commedia actors earned their money through payments made by the audience at the end of—or even during—a performance, in much the same way as our modern buskers. *Lazzi* and *burle* employed various methods for extracting the most money out of audience members. They could be used as a way of inviting passers-by to join the audience, gauging audience interest, waking people up, changing the direction of the performance, or as a commercial break to promote the troupe—all before passing around the hat for money. The more entertaining the *lazzi* and *burle*, the greater likelihood the hat would be filled. These financial responses also helped change and shape the performance to suit different audiences and contexts.

Indeed, it is this tenuous actor-audience relationship that underpins much of the Commedia techniques. Commedia at its best is truly thinking on one's feet to gain the most from a performance situation.

8. *Grummelot*

Grummelot is a term created by French Commedia actors to describe gibberish or nonsense languages which could be used to convey the sense of speech without having to use an actual language. As the troupes travelled throughout various countries where the languages and dialects constantly changed, *grummelot*, combined with gestures and physical actions, allowed verbal communication to take place with audiences. *Grummelot* used onomatopoeia (where the sound of a word imitates the idea or the object the word is describing), rhythm and meter as a foundation to convey meaning. It may have been similar to a contemporary 'rap' routine but in a made-up language. The Italian playwright and actor, Dario Fo, still uses this technique in his plays and some performances, but he calls it '*grammelot*'. Charlie Chaplin used it in his film classic *The Great Dictator* to portray Adolf Hitler. In Australia, the comedy duo The Umbilical Brothers use *grummelot* to perfection to complement their physical antics.

9. Political and Social Commentary

Commedia troupes incorporated the social and political events of the day into their performances. At times when Spain tried to invade Italy, the Capitano character was portrayed as a cowardly Spanish military figure. At times of Italian national unrest, the Captain might have been played as a representative of the Italian authorities trying to suppress the commoners.

Local politics in a city or town might have been incorporated, such as the sending-up of corrupt officials or a shopkeeper who was ripping people off with his prices. The news of the day, gossip, rumour, even local village weddings and birthdays would also find their way into a troupe's performance.

THE ORIGINS OF COMMEDIA

In his book *The Italian Comedy*, Pierre Louis Duchartre suggests that Angelo Beolco (1502–42)—or Il Ruzzante as he was later known (meaning 'sporting' or 'playful')—stimulated the development of local types in performance when he wrote a comedy in prose which was performed in 1528. In his comedy each character spoke a different dialect.

Medieval Players

Perhaps Il Ruzzante was influenced by the tenth- to fifteenth-century tradition of 'the *guillarre*, the travelling comic, singer, mime, who in the Middle Ages was the carrier of a subversive culture'. (Fo: 1988) This prospect is reinforced by Duchartre who suggests another actor, named Giovanni Cecchi (1518–87), won considerable renown by ridiculing popular prejudices in a play called *Assinolo* which was 'perfectly new' in its treatment of 'an incident recently befallen in Pisa, involving certain young students and certain ladies of the town'. (Duchartre: 1966)

Roman Comedy

The interest in contemporary events was a departure from the imitations of the Roman comedies of Terence (190–154 BC) and Plautus (254–184 BC) which constituted Italian Comedy at the time. The closest relation to the Commedia dell'arte is the *Atellanae* (emerging in the third century BC)—comedies, popular farces, parodies and political satires from the ancient city of Atella (now called Aversa), in Roman Campagna. (Duchartre: 1966)

Whatever the plot of the *Atellanae* (Roman Comedy), the actors kept consistent character traits in the roles they played which were reinforced by the wearing of a mask. The dialogue was improvised from a designated plot outline or series of scenes. Characters from this time, such as Bucco and Maccus, reappear in the Commedia as Pulcinella. One thousand seven hundred years after the first performances of the Roman Comedies by the playwrights Plautus and Terence, the characters Manducus the Ogre and Miles Gloriosus became Il Capitano in the Commedia dell'arte. Pappus, the lecherous old miser of Roman times, became Pantalone. These descendants of ancient characters were combined with new types, including the foolish and pedantic Il Dottore, an academic from Renaissance Italy's famous University of Bologna.

The *Atellanae* comedies also filled breaks in the performance with songs, comic routines, acrobatics and impersonations in a way similar to the *lazzi* of the Commedia dell'arte. But perhaps the principal source of characters and comedy that fed the sixteenth-century version came from Greece five hundred years earlier than the Roman Comedies.

Greek Comedy

In the eighth century BC a band of comedians was formed in Karia by Susarion. They wandered through Greece performing their songs, dances, scenes, acrobatics and improvisations. Thespis, in the fifth century BC, performed comedies with music while travelling with his 'chariot-load of vagabonds'. (Duchartre: 1966)

Although he eliminated improvisation, Thespis made big changes to the dominant performance of the time—the Greek *dithyramb*. The *dithyramb* was a hymn sung in honour of Dionysus—the Greek god of wine, music and nature—during festivals and banquets in ancient Greece. During a *dithyramb*, while the dancers or chorus were full of frenzied movement and 'smitten with wine', the leader frequently broke away from the group to execute variations and brilliant steps of his own making.

> The whole performance was something of a joyous, drunken rout, with aimless and wandering steps, uncouth gestures, horseplay, and loud, largely extemporised ejaculations in honour of Dionysus, in prose or verse or both.
>
> (Lawler: 1964)

Thespis revolutionised the *dithyramb* by assuming the role of a character—either 'Dionysus or a mythological hero' (Lawler: 1964)—using speech or spoken verse in the first person, rather than third-person song and dance performed by a Chorus. In other words, he invented the function we now call the 'actor', and the term 'thespian' has been used to describe an actor ever since.

'In 534 BC, Peisistratus, then "tyrant" or dictator of Athens, established there, the great festival of the City Dionysia.' (Lawler: 1964) A contest in *Tragoedia* (goat-song) was held to greet the return of spring and honour Dionysus. Thespis won the first competition, received the 'goat prize' and thereafter Greek Tragedy developed.

Although the *dithyramb* was the source of Tragedy in ancient Greek theatre, it 'remained a choric song and dance of great dignity and beauty'. (Lawler: 1964) But Comedy and Satire also held an important place in the culture of Greece. The *Satyr* performances were, in general, a burlesque presentation of a mythological theme. They were loud, full of obscenities and the Chorus represented *sileni* ('horsemen') or *satyrs* ('goat-men'), or a combination of the two. The performers wore or carried masks and wore animal skin costumes to represent their characters. The leader of the Chorus played an elderly, fat, tipsy servant of Dionysus. There appears to be a strong connection between the antics and characters of the *Satyr* plays and the Commedia dell'arte. After Thespis' win at the first play festival, all playwrights were required to submit three Tragedies and one *Satyr* play to enter the competition. Later on, the Comedy plays developed, though little is known about them. *Lysistrata* (411 BC) by Aristophanes is a good example of one of the few Comedies of the period still in existence.

One of the reasons we know so little about the Comedy of Ancient Greece is because references to it are difficult to find. Aristotle (384–322 BC), an academic, playwright and philosopher, wrote a detailed analysis of the structure of Tragedy, Epic Poetry, Satire and Comedy in his essays called *The Poetics*. Unfortunately most of Aristotle's writings on Comedy have been lost. The contemporary Italian writer, Umberto Eco, offers some answers to this mystery in his novel, *The Name of the Rose*. Eco proposes, through his allegorical tale about medieval monks translating an ancient and very funny text, that the Christian Church may have destroyed or hidden Aristotle's *Book of Comedy*.

Perhaps Comedy was considered more dangerous than Tragedy because at the moment when people laugh they are free of fear and can share with the comedian the mocking of those causing oppression. Certainly the Commedia dell'arte trades heavily on the conspiracy or *complicité* between the actor and audience at the expense of those in power. Other examples of this 'conspiracy' or empathy with the audience might be the Robin Hood story, Mel Gibson's film *Braveheart*, and the Australian films *The Castle* and *Kenny*.

We do know that Aristotle believed Comedy may have evolved from processions of singers who helped to invoke the powers of fertility for the community and to drive away evil. Some of the performances were characterised by witty but abusive and obscene comments made by the marchers to various members of the crowd of onlookers who then retorted in kind and spiritedly, thereby inducing quarrel or contest. (Lawler: 1964)

In her book, *The Dance of the Ancient Greek Theatre*, Lillian B. Lawler suggests that the marchers were crowned with flowers and ivy and carried large phallic symbols, singing hymns to Dionysus. A play by Aristophanes, *The Acharnians* (425 BC), gives an idea of how these processions played out. But they were not the only source of Athenian Comedies. Revel dances or *'komoi'* were popular, hence the Greek term *'komoidia'* or 'comedy'. The *komoi* could involve young men, happy after a drinking bout, wandering at night by torchlight, singing, scuffling, playing practical jokes on one another or on unfortunate passers-by, while improvising dances. A quieter version might involve men marching through town, stopping occasionally to sing and dance to the accompaniment of a flute player. The *komoi* might honour Dionysus, other gods or mythological characters. On other occasions, participants escorted a victorious athlete, poet or prominent citizen to his home. Occasionally reference is made to *komoi* in which the men dressed as women and the women as men in early fertility rituals and dances designed to outwit evil spirits.

Contentiously, the Dorians from Greece, Italy and Sicily not only claimed they introduced women into the performance, they argued that both Tragedy and Comedy originated from Doric culture in the fifth-century BC. They called their surrounding districts *comae* and so claim the word for comic actors, *comodoi*, is derived from the fact that these actors were constantly being thrown out of cities as unworthy of recognition. They wandered from *comoi* to *comoi* and therefore came to be called *comodoi*. Incidentally the Doric word for 'action' is *'dra-n'* and therefore it is suggested that 'drama' comes from the fact that it imitated people in action or presented something done. (Lawler: 1964)

Whatever is true, there is no doubt the Ancient Greeks heavily influenced the Roman *Atellanae* Comedies, which in turn fed the artistic appetites of sixteenth-century Italian comedy troupes in their choice and development of stock characters, the use of masks, improvisation, performance in public places, comic and acrobatic tricks, sexual innuendo, song, dance, cross-dressing, jokes, gags, insults, and satire on political and community issues and key figures in society. Perhaps the Ancient Greeks were influenced by African, Middle-Eastern and Asian civilisations which pre-dated the Greeks' time in the cultural kitchen.

Other Cultures and Comedy

Throughout time many cultures have developed their own forms of comedy and satire. In fourteenth-century Japan, the *Noh* Theatre utilised a farce or comic form of the *Noh* called *Kyogen* which was presented after or between *Noh* plays. Here is a typical scenario:

> A master is disturbed that every time he leaves his house the full jug of wine he keeps is empty when he returns. He suspects his two male servants and therefore ties one servant's hands behind his back and the other servant's hands to a broom handle across the back of his shoulders. When the master leaves, the audience watches the comic antics of the servants who, being tied up, work as a team to overcome their obstacles and give each other a drink from the wine jug. When the master returns, two very drunk servants are asleep on the floor and his jug of wine is empty yet again. This short *Kyogen* play is called *Boshibari* (Tied to a Stick).

The play *Boshibari* has many similar characteristics to the Commedia. It is a highly physical and gestural style of performance based on dance and voice training for the actors. The costumes denote the status of the characters and the setting is simple. *Kyogen*, however, uses no make-up and the actors rarely wear masks. Many African, Asian and indigenous cultures have their own versions of comedy with several elements in common with Commedia dell'arte. It would appear that comedy has a universal appeal to the human psyche.

Returning to Italy

Back now to fifteenth-century Italy. Duchartre argues that two types of performance were dominant. The regular written drama—ordinarily played by the 'Academians'—was known as *commedia sostenuta*, while an alternative type was impromptu comedy using improvisation and masks. The troupes playing this second form—known later as Commedia dell'arte— 'developed a spirit of camaraderie in their playing, and they achieved such understanding and mutual cooperation as were not found in the companies playing ordinary drama or *commedia sostenuta*'. (Duchartre: 1966)

In the 1750s, when the popularity of Commedia was waning, two key figures stepped forward and their endeavours to keep the form alive resulted in what might be called a Comedy War.

Gozzi versus Goldoni

Carlo Gozzi (1720–1806), a brilliant writer and advocate of the masked, improvised performance, provided his actors in the Sacchi Company with scenario-plays which were filled 'with his caustic and malicious wit'. (Duchartre:

1966) Gozzi understood that a good mask-actor was liberated by the mask, inhabited it, was possessed by it and created feats an unmasked actor was incapable of achieving.

Meanwhile, Gozzi's arch enemy, Carlo Goldoni (1707–93), insisted his actors were not to wear masks, did not improvise, and stuck strictly to his tightly-written scripts, echoing the academic approach of the *commedia sostenuta* of the 1500s.

Gozzi was 'violently antagonistic towards Goldoni, often vilifying him with epigrams and satirical sonnets which were models of elegance and biting conciseness'. (Duchartre: 1966) The 'reformer' Goldoni produced scripts full of promise that were never completely fulfilled and he was accused of betraying the Commedia dell'arte and the national characters. Eventually, Goldoni was invited to France where his style was more suited to French tastes. Gozzi continued to celebrate the genius of the masked actor by providing material that inspired, could be elaborated on, and gave the freedom to improvise. Nearly twenty of Goldoni's plays still exist and are performed in several languages, perhaps the most popular being *A Servant of Two Masters.*

Life and Death

As mentioned earlier, the life of a comedy actor throughout history has been a precarious one. The following tale clearly points out the dangers.

The I Gelosi company were playing in Venice when King Henri III requested their presence in France to perform in November 1576. During the journey, the company was kidnapped by the Huguenots and held to ransom. I Gelosi was held in such high regard at the time that Henri paid the ransom and the company members were freed. However, negotiations must have taken some time because the troupe didn't perform until December that year. (Duchartre: 1966)

At other times when troupes were unpopular—usually because they had mocked authority or the hypocrisy of some Church and civic leaders—Church or town authorities were known to have threatened Commedia actors with excommunication, imprisonment or even death.

A Big Leap Forward

While the influence of Commedia dell'arte was evident in the seventeenth and eighteenth centuries—particularly in the Royal Court Theatre of France and Europe, the Restoration Theatre in Britain, and later the Melodramas of Victorian England—it was not until the middle of the twentieth century that the Commedia dell'arte returned with force to the world of performance.

In 1948 a French actor, Jacques Lecoq, went to Italy where he joined Padua University as a teacher and director. In 1951 he was invited to join Piccolo Teatro in Milan to teach actors at the Piccolo School with Paolo Grassi and Georgio

Strehler. Here the three experimented with re-establishing the Commedia dell'arte almost two hundred years after it had faded as a popular theatre form. The sculptor Amleto Sartori joined them and rediscovered the art of designing and making the traditional leather, linen-lined masks. Lecoq, as a director-choreographer, worked with actors such as Dario Fo, Luciano Berio and Anna Magnani. He also worked at the Greek Theatre in Syracuse and the Rome Opera House. Piccolo Teatro's version of Goldoni's *A Servant of Two Masters* is still regarded as a wonderful example of the power of the Commedia dell'arte. It led to a resurgence of an age-old style of comedy that had almost been forgotten.

In 1956 Jacques Lecoq set up his acting school, L'École Internationale de Théâtre Jacques Lecoq, in Paris. An interview featuring Lecoq's approach appears in Chapter 6.

POPULAR CULTURE AND THE COMMEDIA

Perhaps the clearest example of the incorporation of Commedia characters and scenarios into a modern setting is the television program 'Gilligan's Island'. This show explores comic situations involving stock characters shipwrecked on a deserted island and their attempts to survive and get off the island. The main character, Gilligan the first mate, has all the innocent and foolish traits of Arlecchino. The Skipper presents the cowardly traits of Il Capitano when pushing Gilligan ahead into danger, or at other times the 'friendship' of Brighella when he inquires, 'Are you all right, little buddy?' The millionaire, Thurston Howell III, is the rich and miserly Pantalone, while Ginger, the movie star, could be the Lover (*inamorata*), Isabella. Gilligan's love interest is the earthy Mary Ann who parallels Columbina, and the Professor, full of useless information, represents the pedantic Il Dottore. It is a valuable exercise to watch episodes of 'Gilligan's Island' to see how ancient characters still have their equivalents in the contemporary world. Current reality television shows may also reveal the traits and personalities of the age-old characters of the Commedia dell'arte, the *Atellanae* (Roman Comedy) and the Ancient Greek *Satyr* and Comedy plays.

Observation Skills

In Australia, a simple visit to a shopping centre, Sunday market or sporting event will reveal the archetypal traits of most traditional Commedia characters if we observe how people walk, talk, shout, play and interact with one another in these places. Perhaps one's own family may even contain some flavours of the Commedia dell'arte characters! Use your observation skills to note potential Commedia characters in your immediate world which set the table for Australian Commedia recipes to be served.

Response Questions

1) *Why do humans have the desire for laughter?*
2) *What makes us laugh and why?*
3) *What purpose does comedy serve in society?*
4) *What would society be like without comedy?*
5) *When in history has comedy been out of favour with the authorities?*
6) *Why was comedy out of favour? Who banned it? What was the effect on society at the time?*
7) *What are some potential or actual negative outcomes of comedy?*

CHAPTER 2

Spag Bol: Historical Perspectives and Transforming to Australian Landscapes and Contexts

AUSTRALIAN FLAVOURS

There are many different ways to make a pasta sauce. You can make a tomato sauce from scratch using fresh tomatoes, garlic, basil, oregano; or spoon a ready-made sauce from the jar straight onto your plate of spaghetti. And there is a huge range of variations in between. Similarly, there are many different ways of playing Commedia dell'arte. But if we are to serve our apprenticeship well, we first need to understand the principal ingredients that make up Commedia. Once we have learnt the basics, we can then create our own original recipes, as others have done before us.

Everything Changes

If we were to faithfully preserve its tradition in mothballs so that we could only examine it like a dusty butterfly pinned to a piece of styrofoam out of its natural environment, Commedia would quickly become boring, little more than an interesting study in history—a 'dead' language, like Latin.

But Commedia dell'arte is full of life. Like the humble spag bol, it has enjoyed numerous interpretations and incarnations throughout its history. And it is only natural that transporting the genre to Australia results in similar reinvention. The beauty of Commedia is that there is no right or wrong way to play the characters. Actors, writers and directors through the centuries have found new ways of interpreting Commedia; it is constantly evolving for new users and audiences as recipes and languages evolve to suit the times and the cultures in which they find themselves.

The beauty of Commedia as an art form is that it translates so well into other contexts and cultures. And its connection to Australian culture is a perfect fit.

Arlecchino possesses more than his fair share of the larrikinism for which we Australians are famous, and it's perhaps no small coincidence that Pantalone's eyebrows remind us of a certain past Australian Prime Minister! Our ability as a nation to be able to poke fun at ourselves provides a wonderful platform for endless Commedia possibilities.

THE COMMEDIA CHARACTERS

This Chapter provides a brief outline of the historical interpretation of the Commedia characters, as well as parallels to more contemporary characters. The historical information is by no means exhaustive nor is its interpretation sacrosanct. We would suggest that each Commedia student conducts his/her own research into the characters (see the poster exercise at the end of this Chapter); it is incredible how much information is actually available. This is an art form that has been around for five hundred years, and Commedia elements have existed in cultures around the world for eons before this. One thing to remember is that because this has largely been an improvised tradition, you will find huge variations in interpretations and apparent contradictions from one source to the next.

One reason for the contradictions in characters can be attributed to different actors over the ages finding differing character aspects to explore and make famous. Another reason can be attributed to the playwright, director and actors having to continually find the right balance between characters that both contrast and complement each other in status, plot function and context within any given scenario. For instance, in *Stardust* (see Chapter 7), the contemporary Australian Commedia play, it doesn't make sense for Brighella to be the stupid type because that is Arlecchino's function in this particular story.

It's All Good, Mate

What to do? Embrace the differences as possibilities for exploration. The modern interpretations should be treated in the same way as the traditional—everything is up for grabs. The character interpretations we have provided in this book explain and explore the timeless essence of the characters, and will help Commedia students find the 'keys' to the characters, before making them their own and running with them.

It's remarkable how the same 'types' of people surface and resurface across ages, cultures and boundaries. What does this say about humanity? Carl Jung, one of the founding fathers of psychoanalysis, posed the idea that people across cultures generally share common instincts and basic drives. He called this phenomenon the 'collective unconscious'. Perhaps this is one of the reasons why Commedia characters have enjoyed such a long history.

> [Commedia characters] never become extinct, and will only die when the last man on the planet expires. Their host is humanity. They are as much life as breath and heartbeats.
>
> (Tasca: 1992)

The Commedia Ingredients for our Spag Bol

The mix of characters that make up the Commedia reflects the ingredients that constitute the recipe for a good spag bol, in substance, proportion and picancy:

Tomatoes (our most basic ingredient)	Arlecchino
Onions	Pantalone
Minced meat	Brighella
Pepper and parmesan	Pulcinella
Oregano	Columbina
Garlic	Capitano
A dash of red wine	Dottore
A sprig of basil for garnish	The Lovers
The recipe note-taker	Tartaglia

THE SERVANT CHARACTERS

Arlecchino

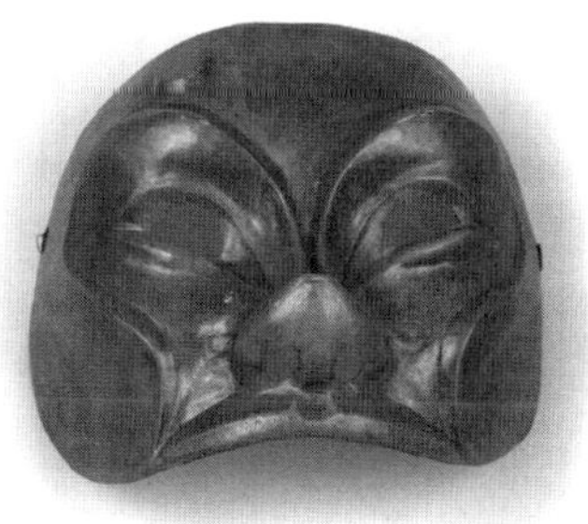

Arlecchino mask by Meghann Montgomery
Photograph by Lucas Dawson

Arlecchino is the quintessential mischievous servant—a larrikin and petty thief, who loves playing tricks on people. His mask is often very dark with high cheeks and cat-like eyes. Traditionally a black strap was worn under the chin of the actor wearing this character mask. While he likes to play tricks, he is often more than a little stupid, but possessing a good deal of cunning in his exploits. He is usually the central character who holds the plot together, the person the audience wants most to succeed, the loveable everyman character. He is innately curious about the lives of others, and a gossip, although not usually a malicious one. Arlecchino is an enthusiastic participant of any plot, always ready for a new adventure. While he is full of quicksilver energy, he is mentally slow and tends to be the last to grasp even the most basic concepts—a delightful contrast that allows for much comic exploration. Offshoots of Arlecchino can be found in France and England where he is referred to as Harlequin. The traditional French unmasked valet, Pierrot, seems to be a combination of Arlecchino, an *inamorato* with a pinch of Pulcinella's simplicity and a sprinkling of the Captain's bravado.

Obsessions

In love, hungry, in trouble.

Countermask

A brilliant idea when it is least expected reached through illogical logic; extreme sadness. (For more on countermask see Chapter 4, p.87)

Relationships

He usually is in love with Columbina but is not quite as smart as her. Servant to either or both of the old men (Pantalone or Dottore) and usually underpaid, which gives him licence to play tricks on and cheat his master/s out of money. Often friends with—or a lower status servant than—Brighella.

Movement

A low centre of gravity; ready for action of any description. Agile, playful, moves quickly, ability to mimic, dance, juggle or tumble. He often leads with his hands and eyes. However, Arlecchino is extremely slothful when it comes to work and will do anything to avoid hard labour.

Animal Characteristics

Blue heeler dog, feral cat, monkey.

Voice

Often high-pitched like Mickey Mouse; light and playful.

Costume

Traditionally, he wore a suit of multicoloured diamonds which evolved out of a costume of rags. In *Stardust*, Arlecchino wore board shorts and a garish Hawaiian shirt.

Modern Day Character Resonances

Film:

David Gulpilil's character Neville Bell in *Crocodile Dundee* (Oz).
Shane Jacobson's character Kenny in *Kenny* (Oz).
Jackie Chan in *Rush Hour, Shanghai Noon* and *Shanghai Knights* (US).
Johnny Depp's character Captain Sparrow in *Pirates of the Caribbean* (series of US/UK films).
Mike, the eyeball character, from *Monsters Inc.* (US animation).
Donkey in *Shrek* (US animation).

Television:

Ahn Do, comedian, actor, 'Dancing with the Stars' contestant (Oz program).
Trevor Marmalade on the 'AFL Footy Show'—always ready for a visual gag or joke (Oz program).
The late Steve Irwin for his high energy and enthusiasm levels in 'Crocodile Hunter' (Oz series)
Bart Simpson, especially with his flair for mischief, rebellion and childish behaviour, in 'The Simpsons' (US animated series).
Bob Denver's character Gilligan in 'Gilligan's Island' (US series).

Other:

Warwick Capper, ex-AFL footballer, entertainer, TV presenter and meter-maid.
Mickey Mouse (animated character from US cartoons).
Monkey, the traditional Chinese character (theatre, TV series and film).
Asterix in the *Asterix* stories (French comic books).
Tigger in *Winnie the Pooh* (children's literature, by A. A. Milne).

Oz Names

Alex, Trevor, Warren or Wozza or Wooza, Gazza, Dazza, Kenny.

Brighella

Brighella mask by Peter Donahue
Photograph by Lucas Dawson

Brighella has been variously interpreted as anything from a cunning, villainous thug or bouncer for hire, to a stupid, loveable, overweight fool who is the butt of all jokes (pun intended!). The *Stardust* interpretation lies somewhere between the two. Brighella has a softer side that we witness when someone unexpectedly shows him love (like 'Sulley' the monster and 'Boo' the little girl in the movie *Monsters Inc.*, or Shrek with the princess and the donkey). Brighella is unexpectedly musical (the guitar is his usual instrument) and occasionally poetic. He is often driven by a desire for violence and/or food.

Obsessions

Violence, cruelty, lust, greediness, revenge.
'I am not a thief. I am an ingenious calculator who finds an object before its owner has lost it.' (Chapter 7 *Stardust* script)

Countermask

Romantic, kind, poetic.

Relationships

Usually smarter than Arlecchino, Brighella is often a higher status servant who manipulates those lower and/or less intelligent than he. Allegiance, for Brighella, usually lies with those who will pay him the most, and he does not suffer fools gladly; he's not the kind of person you want to meet in an alley late at night. As the thug, he is never a victim and always manages to maintain his status.

Movement

He often leads with his belly (the overweight version) or his chest and shoulders or pelvis. He swaggers because of his enormous bulk. He often looks as though he's carrying a tree trunk in each hand. He moves slowly, but is capable of great stealth and grace when he needs to move quickly. Brighella's philosophy on movement:

> Why run when you can walk?
> Why walk when you can stand?
> Why stand when you can sit?
> Why sit when you can lie?
> (Grantham: 2000)

Mask

Often Brighella's mask is an earthy colour with a flat nose like a boxer and small, beady eyes. It's best to present him front-on to the audience because of his broad face and small eyes which allow little peripheral vision. Some Brighella masks have evolved as green in colour, with a fine, long nose and moustache, suggesting to observers that he is an outsider, possibly from Turkey. A hooked knife in the belt buckle completes this version of Brighella.

Animal Characteristics

Dingo, Tasmanian devil. Panther, lion or alley cat. Gorilla.

Voice

Low, raspy and gruff (in contrast to Arlecchino's much lighter voice).

Costume

Traditionally, Brighella wore a white jacket with green trim and full trousers, with a cap, belt and dagger. In *Stardust* he wore a tracksuit and beanie.

Modern Day Character Resonances

Film:

- Geoffrey Rush's character Captain Barbossa in *Pirates of the Caribbean: At World's End*, the third film in the series. In the first two *Pirates of the Caribbean* films Barbossa is more like Il Capitano (series of US/UK films).
- Taylor Kane's character Rudi Kellerman in *The Dish* for the slow and kind version of Brighella (Oz).
- Owen Wilson's character Ray O'Bannon in *Shanghai Noon* and *Shanghai Knights* (US).
- Shrek in *Shrek* (US animation).
- Sulley the blue monster in *Monsters Inc.* (US animation).
- Bruce the Shark in *Finding Nemo* (Oz).

Television:

Sam Newman's antics with panel guests on the 'AFL Footy Show' (Oz program)
Peter Helliar's character Strauchanie the AFL Tragic (Oz program)
Matthew Johns' character Reg Reagan in the 'NRL Footy Show' (Oz program).
Sam Newman's 'Street Talk' sequence in the 'AFL Footy Show' (Oz program).
Homer Simpson (the overweight foolish version) in 'The Simpsons' (US animated series).
Sylvester the Cat's nemesis, the grey bulldog, in Warner Bros Looney Tunes cartoons (US animated series).
Foghorn Leghorn in Warner Bros Looney Tunes cartoons (US animated series).
Alan Hale Jr.'s character The Skipper in 'Gilligan's Island' when he is concerned for Gilligan: 'Are you okay little buddy?' (US series).
Brad Garrett's character Robert Barone (Raymond's brother) in 'Everybody Loves Raymond' (US series).

Other:

Obelix in the *Asterix* stories (French comic books).
Moose in the *Archie* comic series (US comic books).

Oz Names

Keith (pronounced 'Keef'), Wayno, Big Al, Big Eddie.

Pulcinella

Pulcinella mask by Peter Donahue
Photograph by Lucas Dawson

A study of Pulcinella's attributes can sometimes be quite confusing. His mask is asymmetrical with wrinkles and a very bent or broken-looking nose. Sometimes, he is portrayed as a quiet, birdlike character; other times he is a cynical, cruel, violent character, like Punch in the English Punch and Judy children's puppet plays. As Grantham puts it, 'If we seek him [Pulcinella] in existing anecdotes, the information is conflicting. One tells us he was quick-witted, another that he was a dolt. One that he was cruel and malicious, another that he was kindly, sharing his last loaf with a stranger.' (Grantham: 2000) This is because he has been reinvented in different countries. Originally he was a kind character (his name means 'little chicken'), but in England and France he became quite cruel. In *Stardust* (see Chapter 7), he was interpreted as the kinder, quieter character, although (with the help of his friends and a well-placed wooden spoon) he exacted a delightful revenge on Capitano! As with all the other characters, it is up to the individual actor to find the exact temperament of Pulcinella. The good news is that the possibilities are endless!

The contrast in incarnations of this character illustrate that Pulcinella is something of an opportunistic chameleon—a character capable of changing himself to suit the situation. The one thing that all Pulcinella masks have in common is that the features are always crooked, and herein lies the key to interpreting his character, whether through voice, movement, attitude or obsession!

Obsessions
Any distraction, mischief-making, avoiding work, self-obsessed.

Countermask
Revenge, naïve playfulness.

Relationships
Pulcinella is almost always a servant—the varying degrees of his servant status depending on how his character is interpreted and the context required. Sometimes he is Arlecchino's boss, sometimes his subordinate.

Movement
In his meaner incarnations, Pulcinella is often shown as a hunchback, similar to Igor (the stereotypical sidekick to any crazy scientist) or the Hunchback of Notre Dame. He is usually portrayed as agile and swift, but can be slothful if the situation demands. In old illustrations, he is frequently shown wearing baggy sleeves and using his hands a lot. He is often a sleepwalker, which can lead to all sorts of interesting situations, such as urinating on the audience!

Animal Characteristics
Budgerigar, rosella, cockatoo, or any bird from a small sparrow to a vulture.

Voice
Nasal (high- or low-pitched, depending on the interpretation of the character). He often talks in single words, gibberish or *grummelot*.

Costume
Traditionally, Pulcinella wore a long, white, baggy shirt with long sleeves, and a belt to which was attached a slapstick. In *Stardust,* he wore a baggy chef's outfit which emphasised his 'little-ness' and innocence, and his stick was a wooden spoon.

Modern Day Character Resonances
Film:

Adam Sandler in *Big Daddy* or *Happy Gilmore* (US).

Riff Raff from *The Rocky Horror Picture Show* (British film, also the stage version).

Television:

Mario Fenech as a guest presenter in the 'NRL Footy Show' (Oz program).

Garry McDonald's character Norman Gunston on 'The Norman Gunston Show' (Oz series).

Cartman in 'South Park' (US animated series).

Peter Boyle's character Frank Barone (Raymond's father) in 'Everybody Loves Raymond' (US series).

Wayne Knight's character Newman, or Jason Alexander's character George in 'Seinfeld' (US series).

Daniel Davis' character Niles in 'The Nanny' when criticising others (US series).

Alan Alda's character Hawkeye Pierce in 'M*A*S*H' (US series).

Other:

Any retired Aussie boxer in the middle to lower weight range.

The type of kid at school who is good-natured and playful until someone teases them or consistently picks on them, which causes them to explode into a wild rage or violent tantrum.

Or for the less cynical version of Pulcinella:

Boo the little girl in *Monsters Inc.* (US film).

Tweety Pie in Warner Bros Looney Tunes cartoons (US animated TV series).

Oz Names
Punch, Lester, Rocky, Mario.

Zanni

In addition to Arlecchino, Brighella and Pulcinella, the Commedia embraced a whole range of masked male comic servant characters such as Pedrolino, the French Pierrot, and other *zanni* (low-class servants) whose traditional names include Francatrippa, Tonin, Cornetto, Guazzetto, Zaccagnino and Bagatino. (Duchartre: 1966) Often the word 'Zany' was used as a proper name for a character.

Some of the traditional character names have worked their way into the English language to describe oddball and comical people – words such as 'zany', 'corny' and 'tripper'. Most of the *zanni* characters were derived from Arlecchino and Brighella, with similar masks but different costumes and props. The *zanni* had similar obsessions, countermasks and relationships (and combinations of these attributes) to those of the Arlecchino and Brighella characters.

Movement

Depending on their obsession, the *zanni*'s movement could be influenced by a particular body part. For example, *zanni* who were obsessed by food and hunger might lead with their head and thus accentuate their mouth and nose.

Animal Characteristics

The whole animal kingdom is available as an influence on the *zanni*'s physicality. Some Australian animals worth experimenting with include wombat, brown snake, emu, koala, wallaby, kookaburra.

Voice

The use of the voice will be influenced by the movement and animal choice of a performer in addition to whatever inspiration arises from the physical characteristics of the particular *zanni* mask worn.

Costume

There is more freedom for *zanni* performers to choose a costume which reflects the choices made above and the location and time in which the Commedia story is set.

Modern Day Character Resonances

Film and Television:

Andrew, Chris, Chas, Craig and Julian from 'The Chaser's War on Everything' (ABC TV series).

'Pizza', main cast (Oz TV series and theatre) and *Fat Pizza* (Oz Film).

Sacha Baron Cohen's character Ali G in 'Da Ali G Show' (British TV series) and *Ali G Indahouse* (British film).

Kramer in 'Seinfeld' (US TV series).

Oz Names

Franky, Zac, Tony, Netto, Gazzo, Chas.

Columbina

In the Commedia tradition, there are few female characters. This is because, historically, women were not allowed on stage, so all female characters were played by men. This changed over time and the movie *Shakespeare in Love* explores this theme.

In modern Naturalist and Realist theatre, it is usually easier for actors to play characters of their own gender. But if a modern-day female performer restricted herself to portraying only female characters in Commedia pieces, she would find herself limited to playing either Columbina or the female lover. But by playing across the gender divide, so much fun can be had when a female actor makes lewd remarks to women in the audience or other characters when playing Pantalone! Or theatrically punching other characters up as Brighella! Women's observations and experiences with men give them the opportunity to exploit and make fun of male behaviour with hilarious results!

Similarly, although Columbina is usually performed by a woman, there have been some wonderful interpretations of the role when played by male actors who have fully explored the opportunities for mischief and innuendo.

Columbina may be only a female servant, but her character is a delightful one to portray. She more than makes up for the lack of female representatives on the Commedia stage; she's intelligent, sassy, sexy, cheeky, fearless, talented, manipulative and deliciously sharp-tongued. She is totally aware of her assets and thoroughly understands and exploits the effect she has on men, especially old men. She is admired by other women.

She is usually played unmasked, but occasionally, when disguise is required, she wears a pretty half-mask that one might wear to a masquerade ball. She can sing and dance, and is extremely desirable to most men.

Relationships

As a servant character, Columbina is usually employed as a lady-in-waiting to the *inamorata* (female lover). She is often Arlecchino's girlfriend, although she is far smarter and usually helps him sort out situations. Sometimes her name is Harlequine, reflecting her relationship with—and similar nature to—Arlecchino.

When comparing her with the *inamorata*, who is not of servant status, Columbina is far more unrefined and 'knowing' sexually. However, it's important to remember that Commedia is much more humorous when sexual references are hinted at (albeit heavy-handedly) rather than spelled out. Columbina is more likely to refer to sex euphemistically than blatantly: 'Oh Capitano, I've seen your sword and while I agree that such a weapon must be exceedingly dangerous and thrilling, I must urge you to keep it sheathed a while longer. Be sure you don't prick yourself with it!'

Obsessions

Men, control, teasing, justice.

Countermask

Love, belonging.

Movement

All of Columbina's movements are designed to exhibit her assets as seductively as possible. She leads with her pelvis/hips and uses the graceful swaying motion made popular by modern catwalk models. She can move quickly when required and is often a capable dancer.

Animal Characteristics

Peregrine falcon, little tern, gliding possum, Siamese cat.

Voice

Seductive and breathy, literally purring around men, but can be quite sharp and cutting when required. She often puts on a French accent, adding to her perceived exotic nature. You could experiment with Swedish, Russian or other romantic-sounding accents. Accuracy in the accent is not as important as affectation in increasing her allure. In fact, her exotic accent may lapse into broad working-class coarseness from time to time, to great comic effect.

Costume

In old pictures of Columbina, she is usually depicted as a very pretty woman who displays her ankles (ooh la la!) and a low-cut top with a suggestively exposed cleavage. In *Stardust*, she wore cut-off jean shorts and a beach singlet.

Modern Day Character Resonances

There are many modern derivations of Columbina, illustrating her timelessness and her understated feminist sensibilities. However, her feminist ideals are subtly employed and male characters are often unaware of this power. The following are a few of the more successful characters:

Film:

- Eve von Bibra's character Jackie the Airline Steward in *Kenny* (Oz).
- Lucy Liu's character Princess Pei Pei in *Shanghai Noon* (US).
- Keira Knightley's character Elizabeth Sawn in all three *Pirates of the Caribbean* films, although she moves from being an *inamorata* like Isabella, towards the more earthy Columbina as the series goes on (series of US/UK films).

Any of the female agents in the *Austin Powers* movies— 'Oh, *behave*!' (series of US/UK films).
Reese Witherspoon's character Elle in *Legally Blonde* (US).
Television:
Mary Coustas' comic celebrity character Effie in *Acropolis Now* (Oz theatre) and 'Greeks on the Roof' (Oz TV program).
Barbara Feldon's character Agent 99 in 'Get Smart' (US series).
Barbara Eden's character Jeannie in 'I Dream of Jeannie' (US series).
Fran Drescher's character Nanny in 'The Nanny' (US series).
Julia Louis-Dreyfus' character Elaine in 'Seinfeld' (US series).
Dawn Wells' character Mary Ann in 'Gilligan's Island' (US series).
Other:
Jo Stanley (Oz comedian and radio presenter).
Christine Anu (Oz singer/dancer/actor).
Alecia Moore aka Pink (US singer/actor).
Entertainers Jennifer Lopez and Christina Aguilera.

Oz Names

Nina, Sheryl, Joolz, Shaz, Kylie, Nicole, Cynthia (Sin for short!).

THE MILITARY/FOREIGNER

Il Capitano

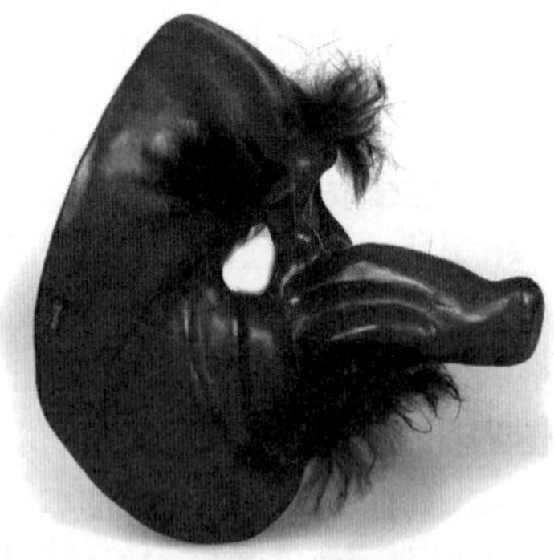

Il Capitano mask by Peter Donahue
Photograph by Lucas Dawson

Il Capitano hovers between the conventional status distinctions of master and servant. His mask features a long phallic nose. Traditionally, Il Capitano was a soldier from Spain (some Italians have a prejudice against Spaniards for many historical reasons) and was often dubbed with an awe-inspiring title, such as Capitano Sparento ('terror'), Cocodrillo ('crocodile') or Terremoto ('earthquake'). His character is a wonderful example of the oxymoron 'military intelligence', and captures all of the blustering self-important stupidity that such a term implies. If we are to translate the Italian prejudice against Spaniards to an Australian context, attitudes towards Capitano seem to parallel the prejudices of some Australians towards Poms, Kiwis, and loud, brash Yanks.

Capitano is your typical braggart who has millions of stories about how brave he is and how many women he has conquered. If everything he said was true, he'd have a life more adventurous than James Bond! But, of course, none of his tales *are* really true. He's probably a deserter from the army or someone who managed to wait out the war doing an office job. The mere mention of violence gives him a nosebleed (and he faints at the sight of blood!). He's never played football but was once knocked unconscious by a stray ball during a stint as sand boy for the Broncos NRL team. He's never had a girlfriend because he has the worst collection of pick-up lines in the world. And his mum still lays out his clothes for him and safety pins a hanky to the inside of his sleeve—you get the idea.

The unravelling of Capitano is always a delight for audiences, precisely because he's so *annoying* and possesses not one iota of humility. The whimpering, snivelling countermask underneath is a wonderful contrast to the haughty, boastful smart alec.

He was traditionally dressed in very fashionable clothes, but so extravagantly that he looked like a ponce, and more than a little effeminate.

Obsessions

Greed, lust, attention-seeking, bravery.

Countermask

Cowardice, impotence.

Relationships

He is usually a friend or associate of either Dottore or Pantalone and has often been chosen to marry the female lover (Dottore or Pantalone's daughter). Of course, Isabella would much prefer to marry the penniless Flavio. Complications abound.

Movement

Leading with his torso and large nose, he tries to make his muscles appear bigger by puffing up his chest. Interestingly, his mask has the biggest nose, and so, in Commedia language, this makes him the biggest fool. It's a good idea to try to show as much profile as possible to accentuate this nose, which is very phallic. He often moves like a stallion, pawing at the ground and showing off. It's enjoyable for Capitano to have an imaginary horse that he loves to ride around on, similar to the Monty Python sketch, or the sheriff and his assistant (Michael Keaton and Ben Elton) in the film *Much Ado About Nothing*. His invisible horse can be easily disposed of—popped with a pin or folded and put into the Captain's pocket. When his countermask reveals his cowardly side, his movement can be mouse-like, cowering and trying to be invisible.

Animal Characteristics

Crocodile (outside), skink (inside), stallion, peacock—in fact, as Rudlin puts it, '... a peacock who has moulted all but one of his tail feathers, but does not know it'. (1995)

Voice

Proud, bellowing, haughty, often with a foreign accent (Spanish, American, New Zealand or upper-class English).
Whimpers, sulks, squeaks and snivels when countermask is revealed.

Costume

Exaggerated military uniform and hat with an ostrich feather. In *Stardust*, he wore army greens with a black beret and carried a super-soaker water machine-gun.

Modern Day Character Resonances

Film:

- Geoffrey Rush's character Captain Barbossa in the first two *Pirates of the Caribbean* films. (In the third film, *At World's End,* Barbossa is more like Brighella.) Also, Tom Hollander's character Lord Cutler Beckett in the third film, *Pirates of the Caribbean: At World's End* (series of US/UK films).
- Kevin Kline's character Otto West in *A Fish Called Wanda* (UK).
- Mike Myers' character Dr Evil in the *Austin Powers* films (series of US/UK films).
- Kenneth Branagh's Gilderoy Lockhart in *Harry Potter and the Chamber of Secrets* (UK film and children's novel).
- Sacha Baron Cohen's character Borat in *Borat—Cultural Learnings...* (UK/US).

Television:

- Glenn Robbins' character Russell Coight—a foreigner to the Outback—in the Russell Coight series (Oz series).
- Kelsey Grammer's character Frasier in 'Frasier', although his explanations are sometimes like Dottore (US series).

The Skipper in 'Gilligan's Island' when acting cowardly or trying to give orders (US series).

Larry Linville's character Major Frank Burns in 'M*A*S*H' (US series).

Other:

The Lion in *The Wizard of Oz* (Frank Baum novel and US film).

Oz Names

Captain Fireblood, Captain Crocodile. Depending on which foreign nationality he might represent: Captain Livermore (UK), Captain Brasstail or Sheepdip (NZ), Captain Chuck (US).

THE MASTER CHARACTERS

Tartaglia

Tartaglia mask by Peter Donahue.
Photograph by Lucas Dawson.

Tartaglia is mentioned first in the list of master characters because he often crosses over into the servant group. His mask usually has droopy eyes and a twisted mouth which could be a smile or a grimace. He is either a low-status master or a high-status servant. As his name suggests, he is a profound stutterer and is traditionally in role as a messenger, lawyer or notary. He usually plays a minor role but is similar to Dottore in the way in which he loves the sound of his own voice and is extremely dorky. If he were a teacher, he would be gaunt and undernourished, wear thick glasses, knee-high socks and a pen protector in his shirt pocket. He would conduct the most boring lessons in the world.

He's a difficult character to portray because the humour of the stutter quickly becomes frustrating for an audience. The most successful interpretations of Tartaglia have been when there's something bizarre about the stutter. For example, the only way he can get past a word he is stuck on is to sing an Elvis song; or he speaks normally unless there's a woman around and then the stutter kicks in; or he gets stuck on a word that appears to be rude, but when he finally gets it out it's perfectly innocent—'Good evening, madam, [*he says, staring at a lady's chest*] what a magnificent b-b-b-b- [*pointing madly*] b-b-brooch you have'; or 'I had a terrible day today, it was sh-sh-sh-sh-shocking!'

Obsessions

Order, clear communication, rules.

Countermask

Occasional fluency and flexibility.

Relationships

As previously mentioned, he has either low master or high servant status. He can be an assistant to one of the masters (for example, when the wealthy Pantalone wants to write his will, he sends for Tartaglia) or can be a butler or valet type. He is usually very shy with the ladies, especially Columbina who sends him into paroxysms of stutters. When things go wrong he develops suicidal tendencies, but even that goes wrong, so he lives to be distressed another day!

Movement

Because he has such a difficult time with verbal communication, he tends to use his hands a lot to help get his point across. He moves very little otherwise because he's paralysed by fear.

Animal Characteristics

Possum, pig.

Voice

Like the Australian TV comedian The Sandman, he has a monotonous or cracking voice.

Costume

Traditionally, he was dressed in the clothing of a lawyer or notary. A modern interpretation might be to clothe him in an ugly suit or traditional school teacher's outfit of polyester shorts, knee-high socks, and a pen protector in his short-sleeved collared shirt or safari suit.

Modern Day Character Resonances

He's the person you meet at the counter when you go for your driver's licence or Centrelink inquiry—you just *know* there's going to be lots of long, boring rules, that he'll take forever to process your application, and that it will probably get lost along the way…

Film:

Geoffrey Rush's character Philip Henslowe in *Shakespeare in Love* (UK/US).

The most boring, old-fashioned teacher you've ever had, e.g. the history teacher in *Ferris Bueller's Day Off* (US).

Television:

Glen Robbins' character Kel Knight in 'Kath and Kim' (Oz series).

Steve Abbott's character The Sandman (Oz TV comedian).

Daniel Davis' character Niles in 'The Nanny' when he is pedantic about organisation (US series).

Porky Pig in Warner Bros Looney Tunes cartoons (US animated series).

Gary Burghoff's character Radar in 'M*A*S*H' (US series).

Oz Names

Anything that can be stuttered: T-T-Thom-m-mas, T-T-T-Timothy, N-N-Nathan-n-niel, Mr T-T-Tort-t-tology.

Pantalone

Mask by Peter Donahue.
Note the unique chin piece with beard on the Pantalone mask used in the original *Stardust* production.
Photograph by Lucas Dawson.

Pantalone is a wonderfully evil and lascivious character. He is money hungry, miserly, old, cranky, bossy, ugly, sly and sleazy. His mask has a very hooked nose, reminiscent of a bird's beak. The only thing that seems to please him is the sight of his precious money or a pretty young girl; the sight of either is certain to make him salivate. He has very few redeeming qualities, although he imagines himself to be youthful, good-looking and exceedingly generous—a real catch! While he often presents as very wealthy, a stranger meeting him would think he were poor; he's too mean to pay his servants properly or to throw out his old clothes or to take a woman out on a date anywhere except for fast food, and that would only be if he get a pensioner's discount. It's always a delight for the audience to see him on the receiving end of jokes and misfortune.

Obsessions

Money, women and power.

Countermask

Unexpected kindness, impotence.

Relationships

Pantalone is a master character—sometimes father, husband, widower, old bachelor. He is often very cruel to his servants. He is usually a friend of Dottore's—either Dottore is planning to marry Pantalone's daughter (female lover) because Pantalone has lots of money, or Dottore's poor son is in love with Pantalone's daughter. Pantalone is often keen to marry his daughter off to a wealthy suitor such as Il Capitano.

Movement

Since he is so old, Pantalone moves with a hunched posture, like a big question mark, with his neck craning out to peer at the world suspiciously. He is usually protecting his money bag which hangs in phallic fashion around his nether regions; he's often holding or absently fondling it. While he carries on incessantly about all sorts of ailments (he's the type to tell you about all his operations in great detail), he possesses great agility when the situation requires it. If he thought someone was stealing his money, if there was an advertisement for a *free* meal, or if he saw a sexy young woman, he will go bounding off in pursuit. As with Capitano, his very large nose accentuates his craggy features and foolishness, so it is an excellent idea to play this mask in profile when the opportunity arises.

Animal Characteristics

Bush turkey, ibis, old rooster or vulture.

Voice

An old man's voice—thin, reedy and nasal, with a harsh, raucous laugh.

Costume

He traditionally wore tight-fitting red stockings and a black cloak lined in red, with a money bag tied around his nether regions. In *Stardust* he wore a white polyester suit with a maroon collared shirt and white slip-on shoes. His pants were held up with a piece of twine because he was too stingy to buy himself a belt.

Modern Day Character Resonances

Film and Television:

- Ron Jacobson's character Kenny's Father in *Kenny* (Oz film).
- John Howard's character Bob Jelly is like a chubby, young version in 'SeaChange' (ABC series).
- Ruth Cracknell's character Mother in 'Mother and Son' (Oz series).
- John Cleese as Basil Fawlty in 'Fawlty Towers' (UK series).
- Mr Burns in 'The Simpsons' (US animated series). The resemblance is startling, even the physical characteristics match!
- Jerry Stiller's character Frank Costanza (George's father) in 'Seinfeld' (US series).
- Jim Backus' character Thurston Howell III in 'Gilligan's Island' (US series).

Other:

- Any twentieth-century Australian media mogul.
- Scrooge in *A Christmas Carol* (Charles Dickens' famous character in UK literature).

OZ Names

Perry Kacker, Miseronymous Toot, Tighty Petighty.

Il Dottore

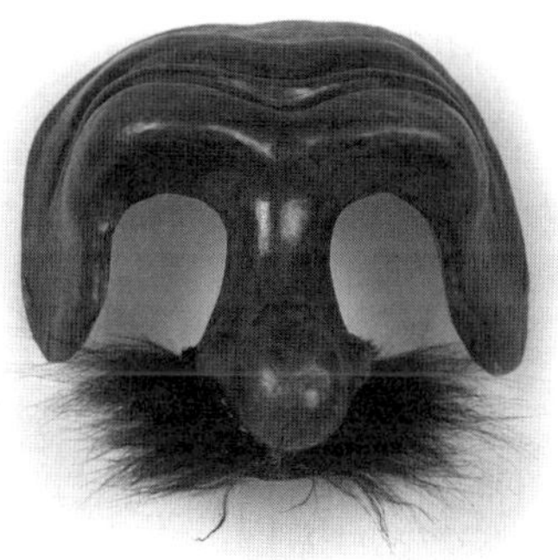

Il Dottore mask by Peter Donahue.
Photograph by Lucas Dawson.

Il Dottore is the second old man of Commedia and either a companion or enemy to Pantalone. His mask is traditionally a T-shape with a gap between the nose and the cheeks in the construction of the mask. He is an academic of dubious origins, a crashing bore who loves the sound of his own voice; his verbal diarrhoea is usually compounded by forgetfulness akin to early onset Alzheimer's Disease. Ask Dottore the time and he is likely to explain how time itself is measured, before digressing to the history of the sundial, leaving the original question unanswered.

Incidentally, a traditional name that became famous for this character around the 1560s was Dr Gratiano, which is derived from an earlier name attached to the character, Gracian Baloardo, meaning 'dullard'. (Duchartre: 1966) The Doctor is reputed to have originated from the City and University of Bologna, hence the reason he may be 'full of Baloney'.

Dottore can be a medical doctor, a Doctor of Philosophy, a lawyer, astronomer or diplomat; whatever the role, he is certain to be a self-appointed expert on *everything*. He is often something of a drinker—this adds to his forgetful nature. He is usually a little more well-meaning than Pantalone, although he shares a few desires with his counterpart, such as miserliness (which is easy because he is often poor, having never worked in a real job) and an appreciation of attractive young women.

Humorous moments arrive for the audience when they try to follow one of Dottore's famously illogical speeches that meander and totally lack a point or conclusion, or when another character tries in vain to interrupt him. In fact, Dottore is usually covering up for his ignorance on the subject about which he wants to appear an expert, and, much to his dismay, his fraud is often found out! He simply invents what he believes to be an appropriate answer, bamboozling and boring the listener with bogus Latin, misused words and ridiculous answers. For more information on how to master Dottore's dialogue, see Chapter 5.

Dottore might describe a servant's fart in fake Latin terms such as 'flatulencio incredabilus' or 'smellalorio awfulsilus'!

Obsessions
His own voice, obscure ideas, superciliousness.

Countermask
Ignorance, impotence.

Relationships
Usually friend, sometimes enemy, to Pantalone. Often father of one of the lovers.

Movement
He enjoys food as well as his wine, so he's quite a bit stouter than Pantalone. He usually leads with his forehead because he has such a 'large' brain and walks something like a penguin, using little movement. He has spent many hours sitting (or sleeping) in libraries and is unused to exercise. He often gesticulates with his index finger when pontificating on his favourite subject.

Animal Characteristics
Penguin or duck.

Voice

A monotonous voice unless he thinks someone is trying to interrupt or is not listening, then he employs pitch, pace, pause and volume to try and recapture his audience.

Costume

Old pictures of Dottore show him wearing an academic gown and cap. In *Stardust* he wore a bathrobe so he could lounge beside the pool all day. A modern interpretation of the academic dress could be a corduroy sports jacket with leather elbow patches and tweed trousers.

Modern Day Character Resonances

Film:

- Christopher Lloyd's character The Professor in the *Back to the Future* movies (US).

Television:

- Ian Parmenter on the ABC cooking program 'Consuming Passions' (Oz program).
- Glenn Robbins' character Russell Coight (especially during historical explanations) in the Russell Coight series (Oz series).
- Russell Johnson's character The Professor in 'Gilligan's Island' (US series).
- 'Mad Scientist' characters in 'The Simpsons' and 'South Park' (US animated series).
- Kelsey Grammer's character Frasier (absolute confidence in his intellectual ability) in 'Frasier' (US series).

Other:

- The world's most boring teacher—we've all had at least one of those!
- Barry Humphries' character Sir Les Patterson (Oz theatre, film and TV).
- Roy in the play *Così* by Louis Nowra (Oz theatre).
- The Australian Minister for Foreign Affairs from any era!

Oz Names

Dr Grayson, Dr Bollard, Dr Mortimer Squiddlyuttbutt.

The Lovers

The male lover is known as the *inamorato*, the female version is the *inamorata*. The male's name can vary from Lelio to Flavio or any 'Days of Our Lives'-sounding names (Bo, Remington, Blair, etc.). The female names range from Isabella, Camilla and Florinda to modern romantic-sounding names (Yasmina, Silvia, Georgina, etc.). The lovers are paired together because their only purpose is to be in love with each other. For the audience, 'they represent the human potential for happiness'. (Rudlin: 1995) They are the heroes of the Commedia scenarios, the couple that the servants are trying to get together, the couple that the masters are trying to keep apart (usually for reasons of money).

They are unmasked characters, traditionally very beautiful, and dressed in the most expensive and trendy clothes of the day. Their manners and education are sophisticated. Unlike the other Commedia characters, they are highly principled—there is never a hint of the unsavoury qualities that haunt the other characters. When not with each other, the lovers are out supporting some worthy cause like the rainforests or homeless orphans.

While they are generally serious types, they do possess a sense of humour, but it is usually a high-brow wit rather than the physical humour that mostly resides below the belt with other characters. Their obsession is love, therefore they constantly depict the typical highs and despair associated with being in love.

Obsession

Love and honour.

Countermask

Competitiveness, jealousy.

Relationships

In love with each other. Often the female is promised to either Il Capitano or one of the old men by her father, Pantalone. The servants help the young lovers to get together and thwart the arranged marriage so that true love prevails.

Movement

They are very proud, elegant people, therefore lead with the chest. They rarely touch one another and are inevitably interrupted by intruders during their secret meetings. A kiss and a hug might occur in the final moments of a show in a tableau or freeze frame with the other characters. A good image to work from is two trapeze artists passing by one another across the stage, trying to hold and maintain contact with each other, but only fleetingly as they cross.

Animal

Love birds.

Voice

Pleasant to listen to; excellent diction and modulation.

Costume

The lovers were always beautifully dressed in the latest fashion of the day. Today it would be Armani and Dior or, at the very least, Country Road!

Modern Day Character Resonances

Film:

Tracey Kerrigan (Sophie Lee) and Con Petropoulous (Eric Bana) in *The Castle* (Oz).

Scott Hastings (Paul Mercurio) and Fran (Tara Morice) in *Strictly Ballroom* (Oz).

Will Turner (Orlando Bloom) in the *Pirates of the Caribbean* films, with his love interest being Elizabeth Swan (Keira Knightley) (series of US/UK films).

Viola De Lessops (Gwyneth Paltrow) and William Shakespeare (Joseph Fiennes) in *Shakespeare in Love* (UK/US).

Daryl Hannah's character Roxanne in *Roxanne* (US film based on the French play *Cyrano de Bergerac* by Edmond Rostand).

Rose (Kate Winslet) and Jack (Leonardo DiCaprio) in *Titanic* (US).

Reese Witherspoon's character Elle in *Legally Blonde* (US).

Television:

Lisa Simpson in 'The Simpsons' (high morals) (US animated series).

Tina Louise's character Ginger in 'Gilligan's Island' (US series).

Other:

Pyramus and Thisbe, Shakespeare's comic characters in *A Midsummer Night's Dream.*

OZ Names

Female: Nicole, Kylie, Adele, Lucinda, Talisha.
Male: Elliott, Bryant, Mansfield, Jason.

A GENERAL NOTE ON FEMALE PERFORMERS

Women in the Commedia generally did not wear masks, as the characters they portrayed were based on the complex nature of the 'actress' playing the role and the particular skills and qualities she possessed. The audiences also loved the honesty and naturalness of the females on stage as a contrast to the foolishness of the men. The wealthier female characters would occasionally wear a mask called a *'loup'* (Duchartre: 1966); it was a fashion item of the day and could be quickly removed or lowered if on the end of a stick. These *loups* or sequined masks, similar to those used at masquerade balls today, were also a good device for the servants or male lover to disguise themselves as females when trying to gain entrance to places that were taboo to males, such as a female's bedroom!

In traditional Commedia dell'arte there is evidence of lesser-known female servants wearing masks and sometimes a female equivalent to Arlecchino, called Arlecchina, would appear. These days, however, it is wonderful for female performers to take on the roles of male masked characters. After all, women are on the receiving end of male behaviour and attitudes most of their lives; therefore, as acute observers of such behaviour, they are often able to portray the male inadequacies of the associated mask characters in a stronger and more accurate manner than many men might.

A SUMMARY OF THE CHARACTERS

There exists a plethora of information on Commedia traditions and interpretations. However, in modern interpretations it is ultimately up to the actor to find his/her own key to the character he/she wishes to play.

The character lists we have provided serve only as a guide for the apprentice Commedia chef and we recommend you experiment with your own ingredients and cook up your own interpretations based on the latest characters to emerge in popular culture and contemporary society. Your interpretations will always depend on the devised plot, character requirements and, of course, the individual personality and talents of the character combined with your own individual personality and appearance. Then you need to add the writer's and director's interpretations to the mix. Finally, with all these components in place, your imagination—the final ingredient—will create the recipe for a character that is entirely unique to you.

While it is important to understand the theory behind Commedia, there is no better way to gain an understanding of the interplay between characters than to experiment with them. The script of *Stardust* (Chapter 7) is an example of the result of experimentation and teamwork, and will hopefully provide you with some ideas as to plot structure, characterisation, and comedic elements that work well in a contemporary Australian landscape. For guidance and practical exercises in unpacking and exploring characters and scenarios in Commedia, see Chapters 3, 4 and 5.

ACTIVITIES FOR REMEMBERING CHARACTER ATTRIBUTES

It can be confusing for students to remember the attributes of all the Commedia characters. The following poster activity may help cement knowledge.

Poster Activity

Students are divided into small groups. Each group is assigned a Commedia character. Using information and pictures from this Chapter, as well as various textbooks, internet and other resources, each group is to design a poster for a character which will later be presented back to the class. Students may even like to work in role. For example, if researching Dottore, the group may decide to have one person in character as Dottore lecturing the rest of the class on his characteristics. Information needed on the poster includes:

Name and other known aliases
Oz name/s
Personality traits
Obsessions
Countermask
Relationships
Movement
Animal characteristics
Voice
Costume (modern and traditional)
Modern day character resonances
Mask illustration (if character uses a mask)
Any other important information particular to the character

When the groups have presented their posters, if possible, display them around the room.

Once the character posters are displayed in the classroom, at the beginning of each subsequent lesson, students can go around to each poster and find out something new about a character and report back to the class what each has learned. These posters are very helpful when a student asks for the twentieth time in a lesson: 'What's Brighella like again?' Just send them to the poster.

Crossword and Wordfind

Test your knowledge of Commedia with the following Crossword and Wordfind puzzles.

K I N K Y S O L V E D D J S A T I R E
C U N N I N G F A Q B U R L E T G P R
E L B M E S N E C H A S E M D C R H X
T H G I N N S T A R D U S T U O O A Q
A L E C O Q O E E D R R S M R M T L F
H D A D I J S N V C E S C I T M C L O
L R D E S V G T E L E Y E S M E E I I
T H W S S I Z Z A L O J N E V D R C R
W L E I E O U Y Z T I V E R D I I S A
O F N R S L B A G G U G E E O A D L N
L W O E B E N U R Y L S A S L H P A E
A F L B O N H E L T O F C O A R D V C
R D A S I T E L N L T S U L T Y X E S
O P T E R D T S W O R D W V I C X P T
M O N E Y E K I N D S K R E N M T A A
E N A S N I V A Q V W E O D R Z B C B
D I P U T S Q O C O U N T E R M A S K
Y P P A H G U A L I V E C M A S T E R
H G O T H G I F S E R V A N T A E B J

actor
agile
beat
bull
burle
cart
chase
climbs
commedia
countermask
cruel
cunning
deaf
desire
director
dolt
ensemble
escape
evil
evolve
fart
fight
flow
foreigner
greedy
happy
hate
horny
insane
kind
kinky
kiss
latin
laugh
lazzi
lecoq
loser
lovers
lust
master
miser
money
moral
night
nose
obsession
pantalone
phallic
resolved
rude
satire
scenario
scene
servant
serve
sexy
slave
sly
solved
stab
stardust
status
stupid
sword
thug
violent
zanni

ACROSS

1. female lover (9)
5. the biggest fool has the biggest _____ (4)
6. thug for hire (9)
9. where performances were traditionally staged (4)
10. Italian word for artist (4)
11. male lover's name (6)
12. body part Columbina leads with (4)
13. purpose of lovers is to be in ____(4)
14. Columbina is very ____ (4)
16. Pantalone loves this (5)
17. loud implement used to beat people (9)
18. chief mischief-maker (10)
21. lovers costumes were based on current ____ (7)

DOWN

2. person who hates people (11)
3. lovers are generally of this status (4)
4. comic servant character (5)
6. modern Simpsons character (4)
7. important never to show the back of this to the audience (4)
8. Pantalone and Dottore are this (3)
9. the foreigner (8)
14. performance outline (8)
15. uses big words (7)
19. comic stage business (5)
20. Tartaglia uses his _____ a lot (5)

Response Questions

1) *Laughter comes from recognising something from your own life. Choose a character you can relate to.*
   (i) Why do you relate to it?
   (ii) Who does it remind you of from your own life?
   (iii) In what ways?
2) *What is a protagonist? Why do you think Arlecchino is often the character whose journey we follow? Why do we identify with him?*
3) *Do you think that social class rivalry in Commedia still holds true for contemporary Australia? Can you think of an example of social class rivalry from your own life?*
4) *Do you agree with Jung's comment about the 'collective unconscious' earlier in the Chapter (p.20)? Why? Why not?*
5) *Are there any new Australian stock character/s who deserve a place in Commedia? Be sure to use the headings used throughout the Chapter (Description, Obsession, Countermask, Relationships, Movement, Animal Characteristics, Voice, Costume).*
6) *Why is it easier to find American characters that contain modern resonances? Are we really second-rate Americans?*
7) *Read the recipe for Commedia earlier in this Chapter (p.21).*
   (i) Do you agree with this analogy? Why/why not?
   (ii) Why do you think Dottore is listed as red wine?
8) *What makes Commedia different from any other Dramatic Art forms you have studied?*

CHAPTER 3

Counter-lunches and Counter-punches: Activities for Instructors and Students of the Commedia dell'arte

TOOLS OF THE TRADE

In cooking, anyone can read a recipe, but it is another thing entirely to actually cook something. Your reading has now given you a basic knowledge of Commedia history and characters—it's time to start incorporating your body into the mix. A chef's apprentice spends years acquiring the skills of their trade by training, peeling carrots, dicing onions, following instructions, not to mention long hours cleaning floors. Similarly, the Commedia apprentice must first master the basics—energy, readiness and listening, physicality, group cohesion (or ensemble) and voice—before they are ready to meet the mask and all its complexities (Chapter 4) and interact with other characters (Chapter 5).

This Chapter and Chapter 4 contain resources for both teachers and students. The activities have not been separated under teacher and student headings because there is so much that belongs in both categories. When we share the teaching and learning processes, with learning exchanged rather than dispensed, students are given the power to direct their own adventures. This book serves as a resource for all participants. Dual ownership of learning gives both students and teachers permission to enjoy, and be challenged by, the tasks at hand.

RELIABLE ACTIVITIES

The following activities have been successfully tested in a variety of settings: professional and amateur theatre, tertiary, adult education, junior and senior secondary, primary schools and pre-schools. While the activities can be adapted for most settings, *all* activities have excelled at senior secondary school level.

These exercises are like recipes—choose one, then enhance or modify it to suit the particular set of taste buds in your classroom. Given that Commedia is an art form that has elements present in most other Drama units, these activities can also be applied to many other Drama menus. They have been numbered in sequence, but can be mixed and matched to suit lesson needs.

PLEASE NOTE:

The activities used in this Chapter, and Chapters 4 and 5, have been separated into categories and coded for ease of use:

- **{LP}** = Lower Primary: Early Childhood–Year 2
- **{P}** = Primary: Years 3–6
- **{M}** = Middle School: Years 6–10
- **{S}** = Senior High School (Years 11–12) and Tertiary

Obviously, some more advanced class groups will want to try more challenging activities, others will need more guidance.

ENERGY

Commedia performance style is extreme. Because Commedia demands high levels of energy, warm-up preparation should take account of this. On a scale of 1 to 10, Commedia operates at 10 and beyond. (Callery: 2001)

Cowboys and Indians {LP, P, M, S}:

Students are transported back to the age of four to play cowboys/cowgirls and indians. They choose to be either a cowboy/girl or an indian. The objective of the game is to kill as many people in the space of one minute as possible using only mime and vocal sound effects. Students can shoot, axe, bow-and-arrow or knife as many people as they like, but *must not make any physical contact with anyone at all.* The moment a player is killed (and, of course, it must be a dramatic death), he/she hits the floor and is reborn. There is no limit as to how many times a student can die and be reborn; he/she can change from a cowboy to an indian or vice versa after each death. There is no 'Matrix' effect, i.e. students can't dodge bullets; if someone shoots in a person's general direction, they must die a dramatic death accompanied by screams and the sounds of blood gushing.

Note: This activity is conducted for a maximum of one minute, timed by the teacher. Students are given a 30–second warning and a 10–second wind-up. Students should achieve as many types of deaths as possible in the minute. This is an extremely high energy game and a marvellous one to illustrate the basic concept of making and accepting physical offers in improvisation. It also demonstrates the level of energy needed in performance and the 'cartoon' nature of Commedia—one moment they are injured, the next they are fine again. The Australian duo The Umbilical Brothers are masters at this type of activity.

Energy Gladiators {LP, P, M, S}:

Students stand in a circle and become World Wrestling Entertainment (WWE) competitors. One person (A) moves to the middle of the circle and points to a person (B) standing in the circle. This challenger (B) enters the circle and faces his/her opponent. (A) makes a violent sound and matching movement (no physical contact allowed) that must be copied *exactly* by (B). If (A) is satisfied with (B)'s effort, then he/she taps (B) on shoulder, and (A) goes back into the circle. If (A) is not satisfied, (B) must keep trying until (A) is satisfied and taps (B) on the shoulder. Once (A) has gone back into the circle, (B) chooses a new opponent, and the cycle begins again with a new opponent (C).

{LP adaptation} Animal copycats: The leader endows each student in turn with an animal (e.g. bush turkey, wombat) and the other students must match the movements and sound exactly. The leader keeps the momentum of the game moving.

Shark Attack on the Gold Coast {S}:

The performance space is divided into two, representing side-by-side television screens. Two actors volunteer to act out an encounter with a shark. Both actors present their solo performances simultaneously using voice and movement, one on each of the television screens. They are not to communicate with one another, but must try to draw as much audience focus to themselves as possible. The results of the competition are revealed when the audience votes by clapping to indicate which performance drew the majority of their attention (applause-o-meter). This is a high energy activity. For an example of this exercise, see Nicky Peelgrane's Actor's Journal in this section under *Response Questions* (p.52).

White Pantomime (*Pantomime Blanc*) involving two characters (played by one actor) {S}:

One actor performs a story in mime which involves at least two characters. The story should revolve around a typical Commedia scenario—a flirtation, a chase, a theft. Each time the actor wants to change character, they must either swiftly spin around to make a physical character change and/or change their eye line and profile to look back at the other character they have just been miming.

> '... gestures replace words because the actor accepts the constraints of not being able to use spoken language. White pantomime

conveys the style of silent performance common in the eighteenth and nineteenth centuries, when Pierrot became the central character, and which is immortalised [by French actor, Jean-Louis Barrault] in the film *Les Enfant du Paradis.*' (Lecoq: 2001)

Response Questions

As mentioned in the 'Navigating the Book' section at the beginning of this book, Nicky Peelgrane was an actor in Steven Gration's play, Stardust. During the rehearsal and performance process, she kept an Actor's Journal of her experiences and impressions. The following excerpt describes the Shark Attack activity (see Exercise, p.51) when it was used during the audition:

Next we played a scenario called 'Shark Attack on the Gold Coast'. The two volunteers had to act out a shark attack simultaneously, as if they were on different televisions placed side-by-side. On one side, my friend Kym Martin performed, and on the other, one of the guys I didn't know. Each unravelled the story in a different way, but with equally amusing results. Kym had me in stitches. Once she had mimed the ritual of setting up her towel on the beach and applying lotion, she went into the water for a dip. The shark snapped at her and stole her bikini top and she was so pissed off—'I'm an unemployed actor and those little triangles cost me $50, you bastard!'—that she went after the shark and wrestled it, à la Steve Irwin, before triumphantly emerging from the water with her bikini top intact, the shark much worse for wear. The guy on the other screen mimed everything beautifully; he was a real 'stud' and was trying to crack onto women on the beach before going for a swim. The moment he spotted the shark, he turned into a total coward and desperately tried to reach safety. Alas, the inevitable and he went down in a glug, glug, glug. What I learned from the exercise is how much energy is required in Commedia and that the storytelling comes from a small part of dialogue and a large part of action. How this opposes the naturalistic cerebral courtroom drama that dominates so much TV (thank goodness)! It was amazing to me as an audience member that, although the physical environment was mimed—from the sand to the beach babes, to the shark itself—I had absolutely no trouble using my imagination to fill in the gaps. This was aided by vocal sounds and only a few words. Afterwards, we had to vote, via applause, which improvisation had drawn our attention the most. Applause, of course, was uproarious for both actors, but upon reflection later, my attention was drawn by humour and gestures I could relate to. I voted for Kym.

---

1) *Comment on the success of actors from your class/cast with regard to heightened energy versus too much dialogue in the Shark Attack activity.*
2) *On a scale of 1–10, how do you rate your own energy (10+ = bouncing off walls, 1 = barely a heartbeat)? Why?*

READINESS AND LISTENING

Much of a Commedia actor's verbal and physical agility comes from the need to be ready to do anything, anywhere, at any time (much like the guys on TV's 'The Chaser's War on Everything'). This means obeying one's first thought or gut reaction. (Johnstone: 1981) Johnstone maintains that each actor has a 'gremlin' or conscience that hovers overhead and tells them that whatever they come up with is never good enough, leaving the actor like a deer caught in headlights, unable to make a 'correct' decision about what to perform. Johnstone's answer is to dismiss the gremlin—encourage your students to 'tell it to get lost'—because, in improvisation, one's first thought is most often the best. Listening to one's first thought nicely complements listening to the offers of one's fellow actors. If we can rid ourselves of our gremlins, we can better concentrate on the task at hand.

Warm-up—Mill and Seethe {LP, P, M, S}:

Since mindful awareness and listening, combined with Dynamic Stillness (see p.62 for more on Dynamic Stillness) or movement, are fundamental to Commedia, this is a wonderful exercise. Students mill and seethe (move about) through the room, observing others around them in the space. Try to have as much uncluttered open space in the Drama room as possible. To sharpen students' concentration, comments along the following lines may be helpful as they move around:

'Be quiet. Observe the world around you. Work as a group. See a space, fill it up, don't congregate in the middle as if you're in a washing machine. Don't walk with friends, you are a private person moving in a public space. Don't worry about other people and what they're doing. Use your peripheral vision to avoid bumping into them. How do you feel today? Sad, happy, tired, neutral? How does your body feel? Sore, ready for work, lethargic, energetic? Don't speak, just take note of how your body is responding to your emotions. Freeze! Take note of where you are in the room. Are you evenly spaced throughout the room? Did you freeze quickly? Action! Work together to fill the space. See a space, fill it up with your body. Change direction. You are ready to respond to any instruction. Listen carefully with your whole body.'

There are many variations to this activity:
a) Ask students to observe one another as they move, looking for details such as the colour of socks, how others' hair is done, etc. When the leader calls 'freeze', the actors close their eyes as they stop. The leader then asks a few of them questions to see how well they have been observing (e.g., 'Jack, what colour jumper is Mary wearing?' 'James, who is standing on your right?')
b) Each time the actors are asked to freeze, the leader can then have them move in different ways ('move as if you have just won a Logie for Best Actor', 'move as if you are a kangaroo', 'an old person', etc.).
c) Once students have developed character walks (see this Chapter and Chapter 2), they can Commedia-ise them. For example, students could move like the Australian animals that are symbolic of each character—a bush turkey for Pantalone, and so on. As the apprentice's knowledge advances, they can move as if they are the characters Pantalone, Brighella, Arlecchino, etc.

This exercise leads into the next warm-up.

Warm-up—Clap 1, Clap 2, Clap 3, Clap 4 {LP, P, M, S}:

Students mill and seethe (see Exercise 1 above) around the room in neutral (i.e. not in character). They must also be neutral in facial expression. The leader claps a first time, everybody freezes. On the second clap, the actors change their focus to look somewhere else in the room. On the third clap, the actors look at one other person without turning their heads, only moving their eyes. On the fourth clap, movement resumes. This is a great exercise in concentration and awareness. During the debrief afterwards, the leader asks the students how eye contact or lack of eye contact felt.

{LP Adaptation}: First clap, stop. Second clap, jump. Third clap, hop. Fourth clap, walk.

Baa Baa Dead Sheep {LP, P, M, S}:

This game can be played in combination with the first two warm-up games mentioned above. Students mill and seethe (Exercise 1) in silence. The leader calls out a variety of instructions (e.g. 'move as if you're trying to touch the ceiling', 'as if you've just received an award for Best Actor', 'as if you're a slug', 'a baby', 'a bird', 'a Playboy bunny'). Interspersed with these instructions, the leader calls out moments to freeze. When students least expect it, the leader says, 'Baa Baa Dead Sheep' and all participants must *immediately* drop to the floor and pretend to be dead. Students must not move a muscle or blink an eyelid. If they are caught moving, or are slow to respond to the command, they are out and must retreat to the side of the room where they become observers of who is moving and inform the leader during subsequent rounds. The leader can try to trick participants by saying things like, 'Baa Baa *Blue* Sheep', or try to find ways to make the 'dead' break their focus. The winner is the last person left.

Thank You Puzzles {P, M, S}:

This activity helps actors to listen and react with their bodies to the physical expressions of others. It also helps them appreciate the power of stillness in Commedia.

Step 1

Students work in pairs in their own space. Person (A) walks into the work space and makes a physical offer that ends in a freeze. For example, (A) lies on the ground on their back with arms placed on their chest like a corpse. Person (B) enters the space and kneels in front of (A) and freezes in a gesture of prayer. This could be the beginning of a scene where (A) mourns the death of (B).

Step 2

A moment after (B) is in their chosen position, (A) says 'Thank you' and gets up to exit the space. In our example, (B) remains in the prayer position while (A) exits the space to decide on their next move. When ready, (A) re-enters the space with a new physical offer. (A) may now stand in front of (B) and freeze in the manner of Jesus on the cross. We now have a scene of someone praying before Christ.
Step 3: (B) now says 'Thank you', stands up and exits the space before turning around to examine (A)'s physical offer to make a new scene with (A). And so on.

Hints: The frozen image does not need to be the beginning of a scene. As with jigsaw puzzles, the actors need to fit together. One thing actors must remember is that they cannot mirror the physical offer, so (A) and (B) cannot both make the same shape with their bodies. The idea is for actors to complement each other's offers rather than imitate them. The leader should challenge the actors not to talk, to make sure they use interesting levels and expressive body shapes. Music can help the work process and, once students develop a rhythm of offers and acceptance, their work becomes compelling viewing for an audience. It is also an exercise in creating a positive environment as actors thank each other for their offers. If actors are hesitating, the leader should encourage them to obey their first thought.

Yes, Let's {LP, P, M, S}:

Students stand in a circle. One person says (for example) 'Let's pretend we're Moulin Rouge dancers', and everybody chimes, 'Yes, let's!' and they all mime the instruction. Each person in the circle has the chance to offer a different idea. Lots of fun, non-threatening and, above all, energising.

Exact Mimic {P, M, S}:

This is a physical version of the Chinese Whispers game. Students are standing in a circle. One person does a simple sound and movement (e.g. 'Hi' accompanied by a wave), the next person has to copy it *exactly*, then pass it on to the next person in the circle, and so on. Note: if somebody cracks up laughing, this then becomes part of the message that gets passed on. Instruct apprentices to never deliberately change the sound and movement—always endeavour to copy *exactly*. By the nature of the exercise, things will change. This is an observation game and the enjoyment comes from being able to copy the other actor exactly when passing it on by listening and watching carefully. It is interesting to see who listens carefully to others. If there is a saboteur in the group who likes to deliberately change the message, other members are usually unlikely to encourage them.

It's Tuesday (Johnstone: 1981) {P, M, S}:

Students are standing in a circle. (A) turns and makes a mundane Offer to (B) (e.g. 'It's Tuesday', or 'You have hair on your head'), who totally over-Accepts the Offer (e.g. 'Oh my gosh, the Queen's coming to dinner! I have to get the best china out, the cucumber sandwiches… Oh my, I forgot to take the crusts off!') Then B turns and makes a boring Offer to (C) (e.g. 'The sun is shining'), and so on around the circle. During the debrief, ask students which Acceptances worked best and demonstrated excellent readiness and listening.

Response Questions

After doing some of the above Readiness and Listening Activities, answer the following:

1) *Do you consider yourself a good 'listener' with body and mind? Why/why not?*
2) *Why is it important to have Readiness and Listening exercises in Commedia?*

3) *How can you prepare your body and mind to maximise your Readiness and Listening:*
   (a) before the exercise?
   (b) at the start of the exercise?
   (c) after the exercise?

PHYSICALITY

One or the Other

Commedia actors are ready for anything, regardless of whether they are standing still or moving. The Commedia is not the place for aimlessly shuffling about in the naturalistic style of a TV soap opera—what is known in some quarters as nose-picking acting. In traditional Commedia the audience was often a long way off and attitude and character needed to be easily recognised. As a consequence, the acting style for Commedia is big, bold and brassy but it is not simply 'exaggerated acting'. Commedia is an amplification of everyday human behaviour and actions.

> Stillness is golden. Slow movement is silver. Quick movement is mercury.
>
> (Grantham: 2000)

If the actor is standing or moving around on stage 'normally', this is not Commedia. Each Commedia character has a unique way of moving, and an important key to playing any of these characters is to find the character's walk. There are many ways for actors to 'find' these walks.

The first few exercises below are designed to help students find their own way into the walks with the power of suggestion. The illustrations of Commedia Walks and Dynamic Stillness Exercises are more prescriptive, but each actor will find their own slight variations because body and movement types are so varied. Commedia apprentices are always invited to create their own interpretations!

Warm-up {LP, P, M, S}:

Always begin each session with yoga or other gentle stretching activities.

Warm-up—Tray of Drinks {LP, P, M, S}:

> Students stand in their own space and imagine they are holding a tray of drinks. Trying to keep the drinks upright, they move the imaginary tray around their bodies, through space, between other people, etc.

Body Isolations {LP, P, M, S}:

Make sure the body is warm before attempting this exercise. The torso is divided into three areas—neck, chest and pelvis. In turn, these areas have three basic positions—forward, neutral, backwards. Demonstrate these positions. Next, have students mill and seethe around the room in neutral. Have them take note of how they are feeling in neutral. Then ask them to pull the neck forward as they walk—how does this make them feel? What sort of character does it remind them of? Then have them push the neck back, as if they are trying to make a double chin. What difference does this make to the rest of the body? Once the leader has gone through each body part and each position—neck forward, neutral and back; chest forward, neutral and back; pelvis forward, neutral and back—start combining the three (e.g. neck forward, chest neutral, pelvis backward). There are lots of funny combinations. Next, have students choose their own combination and, as they are walking around, have them think of an attitude and voice that could match. At some point, have them stop, greet another character, and ask for the time, all with their chosen attitude and voice. Repeat using different combinations.

Warm-up—Copy Walk (Callery: 2001) {M, S}:

Students mill and seethe in neutral. They pair up into (A)s and (B)s. In each pair, (A) keeps walking in neutral, while (B) carefully observes (A)'s walk. The leader asks observation questions: How do they walk? Duckfooted, pigeon-toed, arms swinging, etc.? (A) then follows and observes (B)'s walk. Now (A) imitates (B)'s walk, then begins to exaggerate it by degrees—10%, 50%, 100%. Now they swap. (A) keeps walking in neutral, but (B) begins to imitate (A)'s walk. How accurate is (B)? Could this exaggeration be the beginning of a character?

This game helps students to recognise that movement is unique to each of us and that no movement is ever the same as another's, or truly 'neutral'. These concepts can be unpacked during a debrief after the activity is over.

Walk in the Park {LP, P, M, S}:

While actors mill and seethe, the leader reads the following scripts requiring character body parts to get bigger:

SCRIPT (a)

It's a beautiful day and you decide to take a walk in the park. The sun is shining and the birds are singing. A great day to be alive. Suddenly, your nose gets bigger. Actually, it's a real honker! It's such a big nose that it's weighing you down a bit. You see a lovely flower and stop to smell it before continuing upon your way. You meet someone very good-looking and begin talking to them. (*Imaginary interaction with another character.*) Just as you are about to ask them out, you feel a sneeze coming on and you shower the object of your affections with snot. You quickly steal away as your nose returns to normal.

SCRIPT (b)

Next, your head gets bigger. It's full of big thoughts in your big brain and your head is like an enormous balloon. The wind blows you from behind and carries your head forward as you walk along. Next the wind blows it backward. Notice how this affects your movements. Someone stops to ask you the time and you manage to start telling them the definition of time itself. (*Imaginary interaction with another character.*) How does your big brain affect the way you speak? They clearly don't understand your clever explanation (idiot!) so you say goodbye and walk on as your body returns to normal.

SCRIPT (c)

Now your muscles get bigger. You look like Arnold Schwarzenegger, only bigger. You have the most enormous chest and arm muscles, while your lower body is still teeny. You're very brave and vain and love flexing your muscles for other people. You come to a cliff and are very afraid. The wind is so strong and is blowing hard and you're unbalanced by your huge muscles and tiny lower body. You must… pass… this… ledge. You're very frightened and call out for help. The panic you feel does something to your voice, though. How do you sound as you call out? Do you get to the other side? Your body returns to normal and you continue your walk.

SCRIPT (d)

Your hips begin to swell. They're huge and you're hot stuff. Your big hips make you sway and you've got the attitude to carry them. Notice how this affects your movement. You suddenly realise that everybody has a $50 note stuck to their bottom. While protecting your own, try to discreetly collect as many notes as possible. Your hips become normal once more.

SCRIPT (e)

Your feet become large and are like a pair of skis. How does this affect your walk? You see your bus and run to catch it! Oh no! You miss it and your feet return to normal.

During the debrief at the end of the exercise, have students work out which character each of the enlarged body parts portrays.

(a) = Pantalone
(b) = Dottore
(c) = Capitano
(d) = Columbina
(e) = Pulcinella

Animal Walks {LP, P, M, S}:

While the actors mill and seethe, the leader calls out a series of animal names which the actors must physically emulate. The leader starts with animals from around the world such as lion, giraffe, bear, flamingo, kiwi, sloth, gorilla, etc. and then narrows it down to Australian animals such as wombat, kangaroo, emu, goanna, dingo, magpie, kookaburra etc. The actors all explore the same animal at the same time.
{M, S}: The leader can also play with calling out degrees of *animalness.* Start by calling out 'one hundred percent lion'. Then reduce to 'fifty percent lion and fifty percent human' and finally, 'now just show a hint of lion in your movements'. The actors are then encouraged to choose one favourite animal and explore it physically. The space may now be filled with various animals. The actors are then asked to interact with the other *actor-animals* as they walk around the space. The interactions may involve improvised greetings and verbal conversations where the laughs, words and gestures are influenced by the actors' choices of animals.

Commedia Walks {LP, P, M, S}:

Sashay (skating on ice)	=	Arlecchino
Chicken walk	=	Pantalone
Penguin shuffle	=	Dottore
Happy happy joy joy dance	=	Brighella
Horse stampede	=	Capitano
Sneaky ups (move and freeze)	=	*zanni*
Lovers' trapeze	=	the lovers
Tree-trunk walk	=	Brighella

Lover's Trapeze

Happy Happy, Joy Joy

Horse Stampede

Sneaky Ups

Sashay

Tree Trunk

Lover's Trapeze Exit

Commedia Walks
Illustrations by Benjamin Drake

Split the class into two groups. One group observes the other perform each of the above walks across the Drama room. Debrief after the first group shows their series of walks, and then the second group walks while the first group observes, and debrief again afterwards.

Debrief questions:

Which actors drew the most attention? Why?
Which movements were funny? Why?
Which movements were difficult? Why?
How did you feel during the exercise? Why?

Dynamic Stillness {LP, P, M, S}:

Bodies should be warmed up before going into this exercise.

The class stands in a circle. The leader demonstrates the different positions of Dynamic Stillness (p. 63). These positions communicate to an audience, beyond spoken language, the character's situation in a scene. If the character is in a bowing position, it indicates they are either greeting or subservient to the other character. If the character is in the table-top position they may be disguising themselves as a piece of furniture or betting on ants having a race. If a character is leaning back, they may be observing someone else on a hill or balcony. If they throw their arms up as a variation in leaning back, they may be displaying fear or surrender.

Once the positions have been demonstrated, the students try each position in succession until they feel comfortable holding them.

Then ask students to go through the following movement routine, going from one still position to another. Take them through the positions one at a time.

Begin in a wide neutral stance or position of readiness, then bend forward into (1.) table-top, then twist torso right and bend into (2.) greeting facing right. Now move weight to front leg to (3.) lean forward facing right, follow with twisting the torso 180 degrees left and pivot on feet so the weight is on the back leg in (4.) lean back facing left. Then move torso to centre facing forward then passing through wide neutral stance position, twisting to the right into lean back position facing right (mirror image of lean back facing left), pivot 180 degrees to the left into lean forward facing left. Continue the positions on the left side in reverse order with greeting, then table top and finish in the wide neutral stance. Snap into (5.) thinking pose then snap into (6.) lamp-stand or narrow neutral stance; spin 360 degrees on one leg into thinking pose; then change quickly to thinking pose on the other leg, while swapping arms, until finally the light bulb 'idea' comes.

1. Table-top

2. Greeting right

3. Lean forward right

4. Lean back facing left

5. Thinking pose

6. Lampstand or narrow neutral stance

Dynamic Stillness
Illustrations by Benjamin Drake
Based on Lecoq's 'attitudes' (2001)

Students are asked to think about and explore other interpretations of positions 1–4. The table-top might become a search for something on the ground and the greeting a begging for forgiveness. The lean forward might become secrets being whispered or curiosity at what another character is doing. The lean back might be serenading a lover who is on a balcony or looking up a steep mountain that has to be climbed. The variations are endless especially in the context of improvisations and scene play with more than one character onstage.

Next, each student takes a turn at choosing one position of Dynamic Stillness and justifying it with no more than one spoken phrase or sound e.g. lean-forward position, hand beside the ear saying, 'Shhh! I can hear them plotting!', indicating someone eavesdropping.

Then the students work in pairs. Together, they each choose their favourite Dynamic Stillness positions, each moving through them in a choreographed sequence. Once they have learnt their sequence, they add dialogue and vocal sounds to justify the choreography. This is the beginning of physical scene play with a minimum of words.

Drill for Walks (Grandma's Footsteps with a Twist) {LP, P, M, S}:

Normal rules for Grandma's Footsteps apply where the leader is at the front of the room, with their back turned to the actors who are at the far end of the room. The actors creep up on the leader. When the leader turns around, if anyone is moving, they have to return to the back of the room and begin again. In this Commedia variation, before the leader turns around, they call out a different character each time, so that the actors must move as that character (e.g. Dottore's penguin shuffle). The aim of the game is to be the first person to tag the leader at the front of the room.

Lazzi {P, M, S}:

Collect a number of traditional *lazzi* —*Lazzo* of the Tooth Extractor, *Lazzo* of the Rising Dagger, etc.—and have students experiment with a few of these (see examples in Gordon: 1983). Then have them make up their own. If you want students to take larger risks and learn more physical gags, it is helpful to have a specialist workshop leader who can assist with circus tricks, thigh stands, juggling, tumbling, etc.

A Title for an Australian *Lazzo* {P, M, S}:

Choosing their own titles can inspire actors to make up their own comic routines. Here are some suggestions to get things going:

(a) *Lazzo* of the mud pie
(b) *Lazzo* of the football
(c) *Lazzo* of the sheep
(d) *Lazzo* of the fly killer
(e) *Lazzo* of the coffee club waiter
(f) *Lazzo* of the BBQ
(g) *Lazzo* of the camp fire
(h) *Lazzo* of the swimmer

Reworking a Traditional *Lazzo* {P, M, S}:

Ask students to rework a traditional *lazzo* (see Gordon: 1983) to fit the current Australian cultural landscape. Many examples are to be found in Chapter 7 (*Stardust* script). In the film based on Shakespeare's play, *Much Ado About Nothing*, Kenneth Branagh's character Benedick performs a *lazzo* with a deckchair as he overhears his friends pulling his leg about his beloved Beatrice (Emma Thompson).

Response Questions

1) *Experts agree that possibly 73% of communication is body language and how we say things. Very little communication is what we actually say (27%). Do you agree with this statistic? Give examples to support your answer.*
2) *Why do you think the Commedia actor needs to make a choice between being in a position of Dynamic Stillness or high energy physicality? When is Dynamic Stillness appropriate? When is high energy physicality most appropriate?*
3) *Did you find it difficult or easy to rely so heavily on physicality in performance? Why?*
4) *Which actor in your class was most successful using high energy physicality? What were the most effective means they used?*

During the writing/directing process of Stardust, Steven Gration kept a Director's Journal, detailing his impressions. Once the cast had been chosen, he recorded the following observations:

When I sat down and wrote up the skills that Michael, Kurt, Mary and Nicky had between them I was amazed at what else they could do. To list a few, there were acrobatics, guitar, singing, juggling, German language, percussion, keyboard, ballet and so on… I was determined to use some of these skills in ***Stardust***. There would definitely be music, singing, dance, circus and other languages in the production!

---

5) *What skills do you bring to a Commedia performance? Make a class list of the broad range of skills available.*

GROUP COHESION

Team work makes the dream work

> At its most fundamental level, acting is a living exchange between actors. Complicité (or group cohesion) amongst performers is the crux of ensemble practice, a shared belief which depends on intense awareness and mutual understanding and produces on-stage rapport. Being fully open to other actors is not simply a matter of creating pleasant working relationships. You must be able to work as an ensemble to tell the story sequentially.
>
> (Callery: 2001)

Whatever the unit of work, in the Drama classroom it is imperative to cultivate a supportive, inclusive learning environment so that all participants feel brave enough to take risks. Nowhere else is it more important than in the Commedia unit. Many of the exercises described throughout this book contain elements of successful ensemble. If your class is having trouble working as a team with open relationships, the following exercises may help bring about group cohesion.

Milk Carton Game {LP, P, M, S}:

Using an empty one-litre cardboard milk carton or a small soft ball, students work as a whole group to keep the item in the air. Using people in whatever formation works best for them (let them work it out), give them ten attempts to see how many times they can tap the object around the group before it falls to the ground. The group must all count out aloud how many taps they achieve as they keep it in the air. Some rules: the same person cannot touch the carton twice in a row (like volleyball), the game must involve the whole group, and once the carton hits the ground the group must start over again. Establish records and try and break them over successive lessons.

Debrief the group after the game is over. What worked well? What didn't? What strategies could lead to improvement next time? What is the most successful communication when working together? (Screaming at someone when they mess up is not conducive to positive working relationships!) It's amazing how many students, when challenged about negative comments

toward others, will say, 'Oh, but they knew I was only joking around!' The response for this is, 'Yes, but do you think it helped that person's contribution to the game? How do you think it made that person feel?'
{P} Adaptation: Use a beach ball instead.
{LP} Adaptation: Use a blown-up balloon instead.

Invisible Ball {LP, P, M, S}:

This game is about making and accepting physical offers.

Step 1

Participants stand in a circle. One person begins by imagining a ball and throwing it across the circle to someone else after having made eye contact with that person. The 'ball' can be anything imagined by the actor—a lawn bowl, balloon, ball of snot, cricket ball, etc. What is important here is that the ball received by the person on the other side of the circle is the same as the one that was thrown. For example, if a cricket ball was thrown at top speed, it must be caught at top speed and be of the same shape and weight as the ball thrown. The person who catches the ball then changes it into something else—say, a basketball—and then throws it to someone else in the circle. It is interesting to see how long students can sustain the 'reality of the ball'. Hint: 'It's a hot potato!'—this encourages students to go with their first thought.

Step 2

Add a sound to go with the movement of the ball. Some students do this naturally. A person receiving the ball with a sound must also imitate the sound the other person initiated.

Step 3

When the actor catches the 'ball', it must somehow travel through the body and then be deflected off another part of the body. For example, an actor can eat the ball, then vomit it back up and send it across to another actor. Some of the reactions are grotesque and very Commedia!
{LP} Adaptation: The leader nominates what the object is and does the throwing to the students. For example, the leader says 'baseball' and throws it to a student as if pitching a baseball. The student then returns it to the leader in the same fashion. The leader then says 'balloon' and throws it to next student, and so on. This keeps the momentum of the game moving until students are more adept at making physical offers.
Debrief: Ask students if there were moments they forgot that there was not really a ball at all. How is the use of mime necessary to Commedia?

21 {P, M, S}:

Students stand in a circle and stare at an object on the floor in the middle of the circle. The objective is for the students to randomly count to 21 without making eye contact with one another or establishing an order for people to speak in. Only one person at a time can say a number. The moment two or more people say a number simultaneously, the count starts again. This is an old game, but one which speaks volumes about group dynamics. See if the group can reach 21 in ten or fewer attempts.

'HAH' {P, M, S}:

Students stand in a tight circle with their arms touching shoulder to shoulder, fingers pointing to the floor, staring at an object in the middle of the circle. As a group, they slowly bend their arms at the elbow so that their forearms are parallel to the floor. Any one person at random then says 'HAH' and straightens their arms again, with the rest of the group following suit with noise and action. The objective is for the group to perform 'HAH' together simultaneously so that one cannot tell who led it. Remember, all participants must maintain their focus only on the object in the middle of the circle at all times.

'YES' {P, M, S}:

Students stand in a circle and one person (A) is elected to begin the game. (A) looks across at another person (B) in the circle and once they have eye contact, (A) says 'YES'. (B) walks across the circle toward (A), but (A) must find a new place to stand before (B) reaches them. (A) looks across the circle to (C) who says 'YES'. As (A) makes their way over to (C), (C) must find a new spot by making eye contact with someone else in the circle, and so on. The main objective is to have the transitions appear seamless and to keep the game flowing. Once the game and cohesion are established, take away the 'YES' command and use eye contact only. When it works, the result is a beautiful pattern of silent crossings of the room.

Clap {P, M, S}:

Step 1

Students stand in a circle. A person makes eye contact with the person next to them in the circle, then claps. That person makes eye contact with next person in the same direction and claps, and so the clap is passed around the circle. Make sure eye contact is being made each time the clap is passed before progressing to the next level.

Step 2

Students can randomly change direction around the circle making it go forward or backward.

Step 3

Students can pass the clap across or around the circle, always making sure eye contact is held *before* passing the clap.

Step 4

Take away the clap and students pass nothing but eye contact around or across the circle. They may need a few attempts at this level before it works properly.

Chain links {M, S}:

Actors stand in a line, one behind the other, facing the front of the room and close their eyes. The objective in this game is to mix up the group, then find the original order of the line with eyes closed and no noise. Each actor puts their hands on the shoulders of the person in front. 'Closing your eyes and using touch, observe how the person in front of you is unique so you can find them again.' Students can only touch the person in front's hair, neck and shoulders. Next, the students drop hands and each person spins a couple of times and steps out of the line a few steps, to mix up the line. The students must then try to find the person they studied, thus finding their place back in the line. Appoint a couple of assistants to help the leader prevent students from bumping into each other and the furniture!

Group sit {S}:

Before attempting this one, for safety make sure there is a high level of mutual respect/comfort in the classroom. Students all stand close to one another in a tight circle or line facing one direction, i.e. each person facing the next person's back. Together, they slowly sit into the lap of the person behind them. When it works, the group will be mutually supporting one another's weight without using their arms to hold one another or falling to the ground. To get out of the group sit, all rise carefully together.

Response Questions

1) *What type of person do you describe yourself as when working in a group? Using the list below, you might identify more than one type.*

  - a) *Leader—you want everyone to follow your organisation and delegation.*
  - b) *Hangs back—you wait to be included by others.*
  - c) *Off-task—you are always looking for an opportunity to distract or be distracted.*
  - d) *Lazy—you avoid work at all costs—let someone else do it!*
  - e) *Flexible—you listen well to others and can be a leader or hang back, depending on what is called for.*
  - f) *Inflexible—there's only one way of doing things and that's your way.*
  - g) *Empathiser—you see everything from everybody else's perspective and you have a tendency to sit on the fence and leave decision-making to others.*
  - h) *Talker—you love to discuss things, sometimes to the detriment of actually doing anything.*
  - i) *Blocker—you block everybody else's suggestions without offering alternatives.*
  - j) *Panicker—you don't cope well under pressure.*

2) *Having chosen one or a combination of types, discuss your choice/s with a peer.*
3) *Do they agree with your opinion? Why/why not?*
4) *Can you apply any of the above personality descriptions to specific Commedia characters?*
5) *Do you always behave the same way in group situations or does your contribution change in different situations? Why?*
6) *In group work, is it better to have all of the one type of personality or a mixture of types? Why?*
7) *Have you ever been in an environment where you did not feel comfortable to take risks? Why? When do you feel most comfortable taking risks?*
8) *Do you think it is a necessary part of working in a cast for actors to spend time with one another socially? Why/why not?*
9) *Out of 10 (1 being complete lack of group cohesion, 10 being excellent group cohesion), rate your class or cast. Justify your answer.*

VOICE

Does the voice match?

In Commedia, the character masks are completely ludicrous and quite grotesque to look at. There is nothing less satisfying than watching a Commedia performance and hearing a normal voice that clearly does not match the ridiculous character, movement and mask. The voice is a powerful tool for the actor and is often forgotten when actors are dealing with character movement, mask work and other Commedia features. It's usually better to develop voice and body simultaneously, as with the exercises described in the Physicality section in this Chapter. However, students sometimes find it difficult to coordinate voice and movement together (not unlike the difficulty experienced when patting the head and rubbing the belly simultaneously!). If they are having difficulties, the following exercises may help.

Vocal warm-ups {LP, P, M, S}:

Vocally imitate the sounds of sirens, horse noises, motorbikes. Now put a large pretend toffee in the mouth, and try to chew it, exaggerating the chewing to exercise the mouth. Try tongue twisters such as 'The lips, the teeth, the tip of the tongue'. Have actors make up their own tongue twisters or share a vocal warm-up exercise they know with the group.

Silly noises {LP, P, M, S}:

One student steps into the circle and makes a silly sound accompanied by a gesture that rest of the class must copy. Each person has a turn.

Greetings, Your Majesty {LP, P, M, S}:

One actor sits on a chair facing away from the group. The other participants take turns to say 'Greetings, Your Majesty', using a variety of disguised voices. The objective is for the student on the chair to name the person who is speaking.

This is not a... it's a... {LP, P, M, S}:

The objective is for students to maintain a different voice while thinking creatively. Gather a variety of objects that offer some scope for different interpretation (for example, a coathanger, a chopstick, a Frisbee) and put them in the middle of the circle. Actors take turns to approach the objects and use an unusual voice to state what the object has become and demonstrate a use for it. For example, 'This is not a chopstick, it's a pole vault for fairies.' Objects can be combined with others to create something, such as 'This is not a coathanger and a chopstick, it's a makeshift musical triangle for an orchestra'. Suggested debrief questions for actors could include: Did you like your voice? Was it difficult to maintain? Could we understand what you were saying? Was the volume okay? What kind of Commedia character did that voice make you think of?

Grummelot scenes {LP, P, M, S}:

In Commedia, scenes with gibberish are called *grummelot.* In traditional Commedia, the audience tended to be a long way off and actors found it difficult to be heard. Often, the actors did not speak the local dialect, which is how *grummelot* emerged, and why the actor's physicality needed to be expansive. By using gibberish, actors have more freedom to experiment with modulation (pitch, pace, pause and volume), rhythm and tone, not to mention energy, physicality and character.

Students form pairs and work on Commedia scenarios about love, money or food. Students choose one of these themes and devise a short scene with a short preparation time (3–5 minutes) using gibberish. They can be in role as Commedia characters or other everyday characters. This activity is great fun and helps students realise that communication is so much more than the words we use. During debriefing after the performances, discuss whether the English language was necessary in the scenarios or whether the actors communicated effectively with each other and their audience in gibberish. The most successful groups should be able to communicate their scenes effectively.

{LP} Adaptation: Younger actors do not need to present their work to the whole class unless they are confident performers. A suitable alternative is to rehearse scenes in pairs. Not only does this reduce the pressure of performance, but it allows the whole group to participate simultaneously.

Another possibility is for the leader to have students milling and seething in a marketplace on planet Zorgonto, where everyone speaks Zorgonton, and everyone is discussing how the Zinfast circus has just been to town. In this way, young performers will find themselves using gibberish in an unselfconscious environment.

Response Questions

1) *Why do you think it is important to use a different voice to your own in Commedia? List the reasons.*
2) *Did you find this task difficult? Why?*
3) *Do you find it difficult to maintain different voices during performance? Why? Why not?*
4) *What different parts of the body are used when making vocal sounds and forming words?*
5) *We can change our voice by raising or lowering the pitch of our natural speaking voice. What other things can we do to change our voice?*

CHAPTER 4

Adda Coupla Tinsa Tomatoes: Working in Mask

THE MAGIC OF THE MASK

> There are three masks: The one we think we are, the one we really are and the one we hold in common.
>
> (Lecoq: 2001).

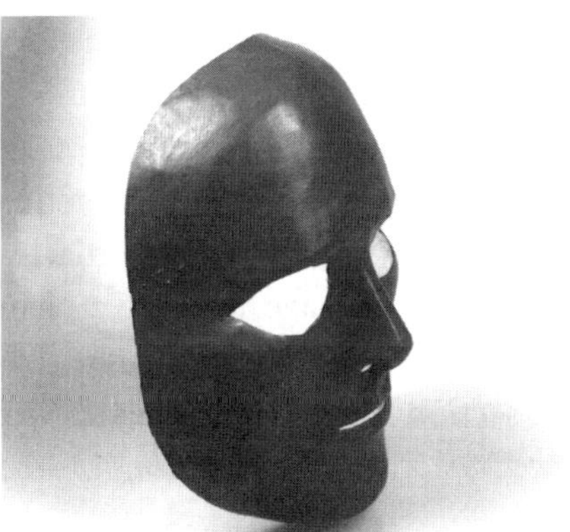

Profile of neutral mask by Russell Fewster.
Photograph by Lucas Dawson

Masks are symbolic. They are the physical representations of the masks we make with our own faces, and use in our communication with others in our society, every day (for example, the teacher with the stern look, the student with the cheeky smirk). We wear masks that we can hide behind and masks that enable us to feel powerful, safe or inspirational, depending on the context.

Since early times, humans in almost every culture have sought to change their appearance by the use of masks. From fierce Papua New Guinean masks to Greek Satyr masks and ethereal Japanese Noh masks, there are many different ways of changing identity. To have an opportunity to work with masks can be thrilling.

Not only do they change our appearance and hold an audience captive, they also exert power over the wearer.

Working in mask can be a strangely spiritual experience and it's a good idea to approach the work from this perspective. It's as if there's a spirit inside each mask and it's going to take over your body—a weird feeling, but very freeing—much like Jim Carrey in the film *The Mask*. We need to respect our masks as something rather special and never mistreat them.

NEUTRAL MASK—A PLACE TO BEGIN

Prior to using Commedia masks, Jacques Lecoq's mask training begins with the Neutral Mask. Lecoq regards Neutral Mask as a 'central point' of his teaching method, and here he gives us an insight into his philosophy:

> The Neutral Mask is an object with its own special characteristics. It is a face which we call *neutral,* a perfectly balanced mask which produces a physical sensation of calm. This object, when placed on the face, should enable one to experience the *state of neutrality* prior to action, a state of receptiveness to everything around us, with no inner conflict. The mask is a reference point, a basic mask, a fulcrum mask for all other masks. Beneath every mask, expressive masks or Commedia dell'arte masks, there is a neutral mask supporting all the others. (Lecoq: 2001)

Training in Neutral Mask is a highly specialised and exacting study. It is beyond the scope of this book to go into detail regarding an approach to Neutral Mask in the classroom. Teachers and students who have access to a Neutral Mask or are able to purchase one, may wish to experiment with some of the rich flavours it offers. If so, we recommend reading the section entitled 'Part II: The World and Its Movements' in Jacques Lecoq's book *The Moving Body—Teaching Creative Theatre* (2001).

Pantalone (left) and Dottore (right) in *Stardust*
Illustrations by Benjamin Drake

MASK TECHNIQUES

Mask techniques are methods of training in mask. As with all types of theatre, Commedia has distinct training methods, just as performances in Neutral Mask and Realism have their own discipline. This Chapter explores two basic approaches to working in Commedia mask: the Aussie Physical Approach and Johnstone's Mask Trance.

Aussie Physical Approach

This approach is based on a mask technique that comes from a European tradition and has been adapted by Lecoq-trained Australian actor Dominique Sweeney. This approach is very conducive to mask training in a classroom context owing to its accessibility and ease of application for both teachers and students.

Step 1

The facilitator asks an actor to select a Commedia mask and observe one prominent physical characteristic of the mask and amplify that characteristic through their whole body. If it is a long, hooked nose that stands out for the actor, for example, then they would make their whole body hook over with a bent spine to amplify the nature of the nose.

Step 2

The actor is asked to decide what animal the mask reminds them of and to then allow that animal to affect the way the mask-character moves, speaks and responds to others (actors and audience). If the actor chooses a vulture as the animal, for instance, then the mask-character would move with a high knee-lift and arms fluttering at their sides. The actor then would alternate between moving swiftly as if in a feeding frenzy, and slowly cocking its head as if looking for its next victim. The voice would have a slightly squawky tone. It is important, though, that the actor does not *become* the animal but is a *human* with animal *characteristics*. The above choices are decided privately by the actor and not discussed or debated until after the improvisation has been completed.

Step 3

The actor goes behind a screen, or into the wings of the stage, puts on the mask and enters, physicalising the choices they have made. The actor has been instructed to immediately see the audience and to interact with them. The audience can talk to the mask-character and even ask questions. An improvisational relationship begins between character and audience.

Step 4

The mask-character leaves when they have exhausted the possibilities with the audience or the facilitator offers an excuse for them to leave (for example, 'I think there is a big bag of gold for you behind that screen'). Once the mask-character has exited, the improvisation finishes.

Step 5

The onlookers debrief the experience with the mask performer taking note of what was effective in the improvisation and the qualities of the character that emerged. Often material from this mask technique will end up in a script and a performance.

When setting up parameters for experiments in mask, it is important to respond to our experiences and those of others with respect. Always debrief after an actor has presented (used) a mask. Students must be given appropriate opportunities to speak of their experiences and to fully de-role before they leave the work space. It is not only beneficial for the actors, but for the observers as well. A good series of questions to start a debrief should be directed to the onlookers first of all:

(a) What did you see?
(b) What happened?
And then, directed to the mask student:
(c) What happened for you?

This brings the reflection into a denotative realm (what was seen), as opposed to connotative comments (what this meant). The latter tends to invite criticism and can have a negative impact on the confidence of a mask student. See also *Response Questions* at the end of this Chapter.

Nicky Peelgrane has reflected upon her early work in mask in her *Stardust* Actor's Journal:

Mask Experience

Too late. My heart thumping inside my ears, I rose to my feet self-consciously, dusted off my backside and approached the table. Part of me wanted to go with a character I already knew a fair bit about, one that I'd had success with in the past, etc. I resolutely put all these preconceived notions and insecurities out of my mind and decided to go with Steven's instruction to select a mask that spoke to me.

It was Pantalone's chin that did it. The mask had a chin strap that had some sort of fluffy rodent's tail on it. My eyes rose to the cruel, beady eyes and hooked nose. I made my mind go blank and breathed as I took in the cruel features and studied the angular cheeks. I chose a vulture as my animal and decided to augment the crookedness of the nose through my body. I know this sounds hokey, but I decided to let the spirit of the mask take me over and trust the spell. I have to clarify this point: what I have just said probably sounds like something out of a Harry Potter book. But there's something extremely magical about mask work. Maybe that's why I like it so much. If you know what you're in for, or think you can second guess what is going to happen, or are 'in on the joke' behind the mask, *it simply doesn't work*.

Going with the first impulse

Anyway, once I'd decided how I was going to handle Pantalone, I took another deep breath and put on the mask. It smelled leathery and bits of it were digging into my face while the chin strap felt funny. I pulled myself together by remembering Keith Johnstone's advice to 'go with your first impulse'; I visualised the mask, adjusted my body and turned around.

From here on, I allowed Pantalone to take over and my memory is pretty vague, similar to that 'outside of myself' feeling I'd experienced during a successful hypnosis experiment. I do remember that Pantalone was not at all shy in coming forward and harassing the poor women in the audience. His tongue and body gestures were certainly very prominent and suggestive and when his advances were rejected by the women, he accused one of them of batting for the other team. Pantalone was extremely sarcastic to all the men in the audience and became sulky when one of them made an accurate retort about his age. His voice sounded very nasal and relatively high-pitched for a male character.

Don't think too much

There was one lucid 'Nicky moment' when I thought about what my feet were doing. For some reason, I was hopping about madly from foot to foot. I had a conscious thought that I was doing this too much for an old man and for an actor who had just been told that Commedia actors were *either* still *or* moving, and that there was to be no more shuffling about the place naturalistically. After I had this thought, the whole thing was in danger of unravelling. I struggled to put the thought out of my mind and not alter my stance. Pantalone exited shortly afterward, having judged himself far superior to all the idiots in the audience.

Back to reality

Dazed, I turned around, removed the mask and smiled sheepishly back at my peers. It was over. During the feedback afterward, nobody mentioned my feet or any moment when 'Nicky' was revealed. I was dying to ask if they saw it, but I guess it's a lot like sinning in the Catholic Church—the moment you've had an impure thought, it's a sin, even though others may not know anything about it!

Now that I'm thinking about it, it probably wasn't all that weird that Pantalone was hopping from foot to foot; after all, he was excited to be in the midst of some beautiful women and he had to prove that he was sprightly enough to be worthy of their attention.

Response

I'm not going to beat myself up about letting my thoughts surface. It's weird, because working in mask for me is not like having a split personality where Nicky is not aware of Pantalone's existence. Nicky and Pantalone are working together, but it's kind of like playing a game of sport; the moment you take your eye off the ball, or get cocky about how well you're doing, it's all lost. I need to let Pantalone do his thing with Nicky *under* the mask, not the other way around. The racquet doesn't do anything unless a person makes it work, but it's the racquet, not the arm, that comes into ultimate contact with the ball.

Johnstone's Mask Trance

Another favoured technique is the mask trance technique. This approach is clearly described in detail in Keith Johnstone's book *Impro, Improvisation for the Theatre* (1981). The technique was first introduced to Australia by David Lander in 1974 when he moved from Canada to set up the improvisational troupe, Madhat Theatre, at Melbourne State College. Actors in this experimental impro-mask company included Margaret Cameron, Raffi Ghazarian, Steven Gration, Johnno Joannides, Megan Jones, Ian Rolland, Lyn Pierse, Denise Scott and Nadia Tass.

Step 1

Essentially, in mask trance technique the actor chooses a mask to wear for whatever reason appeals to them, but makes no other predetermined decisions about that mask. They put the mask on facing upstage. The facilitator turns them around and relaxes them by asking them to focus on their breathing while they stand in a neutral position. When they are relaxed and thinking of nothing, with their eyes open, the leader flashes a small hand mirror at the mask they are wearing. Instantly the actor sees a new person being reflected in the mirror and, if they are open to it, a character is born. The mirror is only large enough to show the mask wearer's head. No contemporary clothing that reminds the actor of his or herself, such as a school uniform, should be seen in the mirror. If possible, cover up the actor's everyday clothes with jackets and cloaks from a costume rack so they have no chance seeing their own clothing. Actors should also remove any personal jewellery for the same reason and for safety.

Step 2

The actor must give themselves over to the new person in the mirror and follow the impulses of the mask character. Often the mask character is totally absorbed by their own reflection in the mirror. These mirror sessions are quite short and the facilitator is advised to stop the session while the character is at a high energy level rather than when it has begun to fade. The session ends before the actor has time to start thinking and pre-empting behaviour. It often takes several short sessions over several rehearsal days for the character to grow and function fully.

Step 3

The facilitator builds a relationship with the mask character similar to that of a parent with a child. The facilitator picks up on primal sounds the character makes and vocalises them back to encourage vocal sounds and eventually the formation of speech. Not all mask characters speak English, they sometimes develop their own gibberish, pidgin English or a foreign language of some kind.

Step 4

The facilitator begins to move the mirror to encourage movement. If the mask character looks at the facilitator curiously while moving the mirror, then the leader introduces himself or herself by name. This promotes interaction with another person rather than the mask remaining preoccupied with its own reflection in the mirror.

Step 5

Next, a toy is introduced for the character to touch—one that will encourage playful behaviour, such as a soft, colourful ball. The toy is placed in front of the mirror and a transition takes place where the mirror is taken away and the toy becomes the focus of the mask character while the leader encourages the character to play with the toy. Sometimes the character snatches the toy and won't share or play with the facilitator; other times it is not interested in the toy; alternatively, the character might engage in playing 'catch' with the facilitator. If the character is not interested in a particular toy, have others on hand to offer until it finds one it likes (a squeaky duck or a soft animal toy, for instance).

Step 6

Finally, the mask character is made aware of the onlookers to test if it will play or interact with them. The throwing of the character's toy by the facilitator towards the onlookers might alert them to the presence of the onlookers. The beginnings of a playful improvisation based around the toy may then begin between the mask character and the onlookers.

Steps 5 and 6 use the mirror only at the initial enrolling of the character. Once the character has been established it is taken away.

Step 7

Every mask training session begins with one actor at a time standing in a neutral position with the mask on, then the facilitator flashes the mirror. Every session ends with the facilitator's hand on the mask character's shoulder saying, 'Stop. Turn around. Take off the mask.'

The facilitator becomes adept at knowing when an actor is just 'acting' behind the mask and when an actor is totally immersed in it, that is, in a mild trance state. This trance state is like those moments when time just disappears. Have you ever walked to school, work or the shops and arrived at your destination but didn't remember any details of the walk? You don't remember crossing the busy road, pushing the pedestrian crossing button, or walking up the steep hill, because you are so absorbed in something, the 'real' world disappears for a while. That feeling is just like mask trance.

Nicky Peelgrane records this trance feeling in her *Stardust* Actor's journal:

Hypnotic awareness

This is such a difficult thing to explain, but it reminds me of when I was at the University of Queensland and volunteered for psychology experiments in hypnotism. In one experiment, they managed to get me to regress back to childhood and I wrote my name as a six-year-old and answered a lot of other questions. Later, I was vaguely aware of what had happened and remembered what I said, but it was as if it were happening to somebody else—all I could do was report on what had happened to someone else from outside of myself. In the next experiment I volunteered for, I couldn't concentrate and was feeling distracted. My consciousness or ego was in the way and I couldn't 'go under'. Not wanting to let the team down, I pretended that I was under hypnosis and answered all the questions. To this day, I don't know if the experimenter knew that I was faking it and second-guessing, but I couldn't look him in the eye as I was leaving. When you're working in mask and you're faking it, it's weird because the mask doesn't actually hide you; it exposes everything and you, the actor, are revealed.

Alternatively, we might consider the trance state to be similar to what the 'Method Actor' is trying to achieve when they get rid of their own ego and *become* the character they are playing rather than *acting* it. The mask trance kicks in a lot quicker than the Method, though. It tends to bypass the censorship part of the brain, so actors often make bolder choices in mask trance than if they had preplanned what their character might do.

Actors have described the flash of the mirror in this trance technique as being like a battery charger energising them, or a switch on the adrenalin pump in their belly kicking in. When they are stopped during a scene or training, they often feel a jolt like an electric shock surge through their body; they quickly come out of the mask trance and back to the reality of the rehearsal room.

Advanced Mask Work

Step 8

After an actor has worked in the same mask over several mask trance sessions, the leader can call up two actors to work at the same time. The facilitator quickly gives each mask character a flash of the mirror, in the manner described above, and makes each character aware of the other by verbally prompting, 'Hey, who's your friend over there? Do you know them?'

The process of two (or more) mask trance characters working at the same time trains the actors in the nature of group cohesion and playful interactions with one another—*complicité*.

The facilitator must be alert, working quickly to call, 'Stop. Turn around. Take off the mask', if any unsafe situations arise (such as climbing out windows) or if one or more of the characters behaves violently. After several sessions, the command to 'Stop. Turn around. Take off the mask' should be enough to break the trance without the need for the facilitator to place a hand on a participant's shoulder.

Step 9

Oncc actors are familiar with wearing one particular mask, often just the feel of the mask will ignite the character when the mask is put on, without the use of the mirror. It's a bit like putting on a pair of tap shoes—the body knows instinctively what to do.

Some actors find that key words or sounds emerge from a particular mask character during mask trance training. They may simply put on the mask and repeat these key words or sounds for the character to come alive. Alternatively, an actor may have discovered a specific toy or prop that their mask character loves and, after putting on the mask, all the actor needs to do is pick up that toy or prop for the mask character to spring into life. For example, the actor putting on the Pantalone mask and picking up a cloth bag full of coins is enough to spur Pantalone into action.

Teachers, directors and facilitators should decide for themselves how confident they feel about introducing the mask trance approach into the classroom, workshops or performance. We highly recommend Johnstone's chapter on 'Masks and Trance' for a detailed explanation of the concepts, philosophy and application of mask trance work.

Nicky Peelgrane responds in her journal to mask trance during rehearsal for *Stardust*:

My Experience:

When it was my turn, I chose the Dottore mask. I felt very nervous after watching a few other actors go through the experience with the most incredible results. Characters were very base and animal-like; I could relate to them being more like animals or babies rather than adult humans. But I guess this is the Commedia tradition, it strips away sophisticated civilisation and exposes the animal drive hidden within all of us. Anyway, I put on the mask with my back to the audience, closed my eyes and breathed, then at the top of the inward breath, I opened them and was astonished to see the creature in front of me. I forgot about how Dottore 'should' sound, move, etc. and stared at the new me as if I were a kangaroo frozen in the headlights. Somewhere from inside of me came a 'Hunh', as if the character were responding to a blow to the stomach. Steven echoed this noise from behind the mirror and the character realised that this sound pleased him and then repeated it. This then became a game of sound imitation—the character would initiate an animal sound, then Steven would repeat or vary it. Suddenly, the mirror dropped down from view. The character was vain and liked looking at himself and so tried to find the mirror. This became a game of chasing the mirror with the tenor 'Hunh' of the character expressing delight.

Unexpectedly, the mirror was gone. Indignant, the character searched for it, but to no avail. Instead, he was handed an egg shaker. A deep 'Ooooooh' was the response as he grabbed it and, as if he'd never seen one before, began playing with it, shaking it, discovering how it worked. The shaking sound pleased him very much. Then he noticed the audience watching and it became an opportunity to show off. What could he do with the shaker next to build on the game? He thought himself very funny and clever when he put it down his pants and started jumping up and down, laughing at the sound of the shaker inside his duds. Next thing I hear Steven say, 'Stop. Turn around. Take off the mask.'

Response

Wow! Where did that come from?! I could really understand why it was called 'Mask Trance'! All of my personality, ego, intellect and emotional baggage were completely stripped away and it was as if I had gone back to early childhood or perhaps regressed in the evolutionary progression to Neanderthal status. As I sat back down, I became aware that the others in the cast had been laughing throughout the experiment; evidently, a shaker down the daks is funny stuff (not merely for the character)... It was as if I had regressed to childhood, but I think this childish fascination with things is characteristic of Commedia. A friend of mine the other day was telling me about her two-year-old daughter who could see the pattern of fish on her father's shirt. 'Fish! Fish!' she exclaimed, as if she'd never seen a fish on a shirt before. 'Daddy's got a fish!' she shrieked with delight, over and over. It's that same kind of innocently engaging enthusiasm and energy that we find so captivating about young children that helps define Commedia characters.

Upon further reflection, I realised how different from the traditional voluble Dottore my character was. But Steven explained that using mask trance takes the character back to its very foundations. He said that during the rehearsal process the characters would grow up and progress via the trance technique to being (mostly) coherent adults. What an incredible process.

PROPS AND COSTUMING HINTS

When actors are just beginning to work in mask, and while they're still learning to obey basic impulses, it's a good idea to have a number of simple objects on hand for them to explore individually, such as a small bean bag, egg beater etc. Childlike interaction with the object while in mask is fascinating to watch and unleashes many possibilities while, at the same time, the actors become more comfortable in the mask.

Keep a collection of hats and scarves on hand to assist with character building and mask work. It's amazing how a hat can assist a character's attitude. Also, keep a number of small sponges or felt on hand to be placed under the masks so that they are not digging too much into the students' faces—it's difficult to sustain character when the mask keeps cutting into your eye, or slipping down your face. Don't feel the need to keep students continually working in mask throughout the unit—it's difficult and exhausting work. However, by the time they start to reach the synthesising stage of their learning, you can keep them in mask more frequently and for longer periods. If more than one student is to use the same mask in a session, it's a good idea for leaders to have some spray disinfectant and paper towels on hand to maintain hygiene amongst mask wearers.

With props, try to keep them simple. It's handy to have props that serve a variety of purposes. A wooden spoon can be used for stirring things, a conductor's baton, a gun, a sword, an implement for wreaking havoc and revenge. Students can become bamboozled and distracted by too many props and intricate costumes. The session becomes a fashion parade or a logistical exercise, whereas the focus should be solely on the action itself.

MASK PROTOCOLS

We must have respect for the masks and the magic they possess; we must never mistreat them. There are some universally accepted 'rules' that are worth mentioning when using masks. These apply to Commedia dell'arte and many other forms of mask performance across a variety of cultures.

The actor should never put the mask on in front of onlookers or an audience. They should go behind a screen upstage or into the theatre wings so that they can enter the performance space with the mask already on. If neither a screen nor wings are available, the actor may turn upstage, away from onlookers, to put the mask in place. Once the mask is on, the actor never touches the mask again, or any other actor's mask, until the improvisation, scene or performance is over. The mask character must exit before the actor takes off the mask or, if no exit is possible, turn upstage, away from onlookers or audience, to remove the mask.

Taking off or touching the mask in character can break the illusion of performance. There's a story that exists as part of Australian mask folklore that describes the children's TV character Humphrey B. Bear, who is played by an actor in a full bear suit. When on set, filming a show before a live audience, a bee got stuck inside the head of the bear. The actor, not wanting to be stung, reacted by ripping the head off and booting it over the heads of the astonished children in the audience; forty four-year-olds in turn reacted with screams and hysterical crying. Until that moment they thought Humphrey was real! This is an extreme example, but one that students will remember.

If the mask accidentally slips or is knocked crooked during performance, and the actor can't find an excuse for their character to exit to adjust the mask offstage, once again they should turn upstage to fix the problem.

A mask is never stored face down, never left on the floor or thrown around. This ensures the mask won't be accidentally trodden on, damaged or scratched, and it shows respect for it as an actor's tool. Some cultures regard the mask as sacred. A mask that is meant for performance should never be worn as a joke or a fancy dress costume. There are plenty of other cheap masks for putting on the wall or to wear at parties, but masks intended for theatrical or cultural performances should never be used in this way!

In performance or improvisations (even in mask trance) a tiny part of the actor monitors what their character is doing to avoid accidents and to ensure the back of the character is not showing for any length of time. The sight of the back of a head and the elastic holding the mask in place is not very conducive to mask performance, especially in Commedia dell'arte. The masks are at their strongest when they are presented front-on to an audience or in profile. The back of the head should only be seen in transitional moves such as when dancing, doing tumbles and acrobatics or physical comic business like being kicked up the butt! Even exits should be engineered or choreographed to see as much of the mask as possible before the character disappears. This is generally not a problem for Commedia mask characters because they are so egotistical and have such a wonderful love/hate relationship with their audience that they are constantly making eye contact, if not physical contact, with their audience.

Mask Protocols Summary

Offstage and in training:

1) Always store masks safely so they are not trodden on or thrown around.
2) Never swing a mask around when not in use or push it up on the forehead. This shows disrespect for the mask.
3) A mask meant for theatrical or cultural performance should never be worn as a joke or fancy costume.
4) Always keep masks facing upward when not in use, otherwise delicate paint may chip or the surface may be scuffed.

On stage and in performance:

1) Don't put a mask on in front of an audience. A performer must put it on either offstage or with their back to the audience.
2) Try never to touch the mask you are wearing (or anyone else's mask) during performance. The audience should never be reminded that the actor is wearing a mask.
3) Never adjust a mask in front of the audience. If the mask slips or is cutting into the face or eyes, stop, turn around, fix the problem, then face the audience again. Don't turn around to the audience until you're in character.
4) Try to not show the back of the mask (i.e. elastic or strings) to the audience when in character (see the following exercises on Dog Poo and Obstacle Course). Actors need to learn the acting space by touch, especially when masks don't allow peripheral vision.
5) Masks are at their strongest when they are front-on to an audience or in profile (see the Dog Poo exercise below).
6) Never take off a mask in front of an audience. Otherwise, the illusion is broken.
7) Exits should be engineered or choreographed to see as much of the mask as possible before the character disappears.

Mask Protocol Exercises

Dog Poo {P, M, S}:

Some Commedia masks, especially large-nosed characters such as Pantalone and Capitano, are more effective in profile to the audience. Other masks, such as Arlecchino and Brighella, are better suited face-on to the audience. A way of getting students to keep this in mind and to help them remember that much of Commedia is about connecting with the audience directly, is to try the Dog Poo exercise.

One at a time, actors cross the stage in character and mask, with their eyes focused on the facilitator who stands as if in the audience. No matter what the body does, the actor must always keep their eyes, and therefore the mask, focused on the leader. The actor steps in dog poo halfway across the stage, the facilitator making a raspberry noise to signify stepping in the poo. Then the actor must react to the poo without changing facial expression or face direction and keep looking forward with their eyes locked on the leader while progressing to exit on the other side of the stage. For example, the actor may decide to try and wipe the poo off on the floor.

The reaction is physical, not facial, and serves to remind the actor of three things: that facial expression is redundant behind a mask; that Commedia trades heavily on the actor/audience connection; and, thirdly, that masks look best when fully facing the audience.

Obstacle Course {P, M, S}:

Another way to help actors avoid showing the backs of their masks to an audience is to set up an obstacle course. The actor begins downstage facing the audience, with the obstacles set upstage of them. They are allowed one quick glance behind to take in the obstacle course before making their way backwards, avoiding all the objects, until they can make an exit upstage. They must remain facing forward at all times. If they bump into any objects, then they must justify it with dialogue or attitude. The secret is to react to everything. Make sure Work Place Health and Safety 'common sense' applies—no objects that may injure some poor actor!

Nicky Peelgrane details examples of playing with objects and character interactions in her *Stardust* Actor's journal:

We've been doing a lot of mask work. Even though it's very draining (I don't know how I'm going to manage a whole performance in mask—we're only working for a few minutes at a time at this stage), it's really interesting. Initially we did some work with our characters similar to those experiences in the audition. Now we've progressed to playing with small toys on our own similar to the egg shaker I described earlier. We've laughed that anybody walking into our rehearsal room would think that this was a day care centre for regressed adults. It's made me think back to my nannying days when I observed small children and infants discovering something we adults perceive as commonplace. A rattle or jar of dried pasta can engage children for hours as they experiment and discover.

Recently the characters began interacting with each other. We find that characters play together beautifully for a limited time before the usual jealousies over toys or food erupt. *'Mine!'* is a common word to accompany the familiar tussles. I can understand now how the characters will grow up and I can see where Steven is heading with the interplay. The child/animal-like qualities will recede somewhat as some adult qualities take over. It's like doing a life history in fast forward—I'm sure the process will make for a more three-dimensional character in the end.

At the end of a day's mask work, I'm always left with these questions. How much is the actor and how much is the mask? How much is conscious? How much is following the instinct of the mask? How do you remember what the mask looks like when it's on your face? How do you know when to finish? How was I going to react to another mask character? I'm thinking too much, I can tell…

Countermask

We have mentioned the idea of countermask and status reversal in Commedia in Chapters 1 and 2. Each character is driven by an obsession and demonstrates typical traits. For instance, Brighella is a thug for hire, and his loyalty lies with the person who pays the most (think of Samuel L. Jackson's character, Jules Winnfield, in the movie *Pulp Fiction*). But when we see the other side of Brighella and someone shows him unexpected kindness or trust, we see his countermask qualities—he really is a softie underneath and behaves like a big kid. In the *Pulp Fiction* example, when Jules Winnfield and Vincent Vega are having a trivial conversation about 'Royale with Cheese' burgers, they are not behaving like thugs at that moment. The audience briefly sees another side to them. This lighter moment is a contrast to the brutality in the violent scenes that follow. It makes the characters more endearing, realistic, interesting and likeable to the audience. If we only get to see their thuggish side, they remain as stereotypes, and we're less interested in their story because we've seen one-dimensional characters like them so many times before.

Response Questions

1) *After working in mask, answer the following questions:*
2) *Which mask did you choose and why?*
3) *What mask features did you express/amplify through your body?*
4) *Did you follow mask protocols properly? If not, what areas do you need to improve upon?*
5) *Dymphna Callery believes that 'Mask work becomes an exercise in honesty. It is always apparent when movement is false—you 'see' the actor beneath the mask. When it is honest, mask and actor seem fused into utterly convincing character. (Callery: 2001) How did you feel during the mask work? Were there any lucid 'You' moments, that is, moments when the actor was revealed rather than the mask character? If so, what caused these to happen?*
6) *As an audience member, were there any moments you can identify when other actors in mask were 'honest', that is, the mask character was utterly convincing? What effect did it have upon the audience?*
7) *Do you like mask work? Why/why not?*
8) *With the benefit of reflection, how could you have improved your time on stage in mask?*
9) *What do you know of Neutral Mask, Larval Mask, or other masks used in rituals, dances or performance?*

CHAPTER 5

Welcome to Da Family: Playing with other Commedia Characters

Once the apprentice chef has learned the basics and become proficient at cooking a variety of foods, it's time to begin experimenting with recipes of their own. Similarly, the apprentice theatre maker is now ready to experiment with new ingredients and devise their own Commedia recipes. By the end of this Chapter, students will be devising their own *canovacci* (see Chapter 1). *Canovacci* might sound like a recipe for pasta, but, in fact, a *canovacci* ('scene list') is more like a recipe for actors. It's a set of instructions—a step-by-step outline for a short performance that contains essential Commedia ingredients.

From very simple scenarios to more elaborate twists and trysts, apprentices in this section will begin experimenting with other Commedia family members in servant/master relationships; embarking on the complexities of countermask, *burle*, music and singing; and finally putting it all together into scenarios.

STATUS

> Social animals have inbuilt rules which prevent them from killing one another for food, mates and so on. These animals will, however, confront each other, and sometimes fight, until a hierarchy is established, after which there is no fighting unless an attempt is made to change the 'pecking order'. This system is found in animals as diverse as human beings, chickens and woodlice.
>
> (Johnstone: 1981)

In a theatrical context this 'pecking order' is called 'status'. The status of a character can change from very high (Pantalone, a master) to very low (Arlecchino, a servant). In the Commedia, status transactions are constantly occurring and status reversals often take place. At the end of a Commedia performance, Arlecchino may well be at the top of the pecking order and Pantalone in the middle or even at the bottom.

As with humans, Commedia characters establish their status by what they do and say. For example, the duties of a king might seem to give them high status, but if the court jester is making 'rabbit ears' behind the king's head, causing onlookers to laugh, then the jester has the higher status for that moment. If the jester is caught making a fool of the king he may be sent to his execution and, therefore, as a dead jester his status has become very low indeed! If the jester returns as a ghost to haunt and torment the king, however, then the jester once again has higher status than the king.

Servant/Master Relationships

Much of the conflict in Commedia exists between the servants and masters. Masks are usually divided into three distinct groups with the fourth group, the Lovers, remaining unmasked, although there are many variations. The groups are:

Masters	Pantalone, Dottore, Tartaglia (who is sometimes a servant)
Foreigner	Il Capitano (Spanish, but in an Aussie context, think American)
Servants	Pulcinella, Arlecchino, Brighella, Columbina, other *zanni*
Lovers	*inamorata*, *inamorato*

(For more information on each of the characters, see Chapter 2.)

Most scenarios are based on tensions between servants (oppressed, although sometimes oppressors themselves) and masters (oppressors). The tension is driven by not knowing who is going to win the fight.

Simple Status or Status Battles {P, M, S}:

Step 1

Two unmasked players are asked to sit in chairs side by side in neutral status facing the audience. When the leader claps, the players must each sit on their chair in a way that displays high status. They cannot talk or have physical contact with each other. Just by the way they sit they are trying to be high status or 'very important'. Once they are in their chosen sitting position the leader tells them to freeze. The audience then analyses and discusses for a minute who they think has the highest status.

Do not be seduced by the player who crosses their arms or legs or pulls an angry face. This is defensive/aggressive behaviour and signals insecurity rather than high status.

Step 2

Two new players begin a high status battle sitting on the seats, but this time they are allowed to stand and move off the seat if it helps them gain status. They too cannot talk or have physical contact with one another. Once again the players freeze and the audience gives feedback on who is winning the status battle. The players may be instructed to continue and try different tactics suggested by the audience.

A player may use height over the other player, block them by standing in front of them or even make fun of them behind their back.

Step 3:

Two new players begin by sitting. They may stand and move and talk and have physical contact with one another if it helps attain high status. They can talk to each other, to imaginary others (servants, etc.) or to the audience, but only if it gains them status.

Be wary of the player who wants to use physical violence. High status people delegate and do not get their own hands dirty with such activities. More often they use gesture and words to intimidate or get what they want.

By now the audience should begin to recognise the qualities of the high status person:

- Takes up space with their body.
- Balanced, earthed, symmetrical body shapes.
- Stillness.
- Openly engages the world with their eyes and is content to be looked at.
- Relaxed body and face.
- Direct, efficient movements and gestures.
- Uses language efficiently, mostly making statements or giving commands.
- Speaks clearly but neither too loudly or too softly.
- Uses strong stage positions eg Downstage Centre (DSC).

The battle for low status can be played in the same three steps as above. The qualities of the low status person include:

- Takes up as little space as possible or becomes 'invisible'.
- Unbalanced, unearthed, asymmetrical (contorted) body shapes.
- Restless and fidgety energy.
- Avoids eye contact with the world and hides their face to avoid being looked at.
- Lots of tension in the body and face.
- Indirect, inefficient movement and gestures.
- Uses language inefficiently (babbling and rambling on), mostly asking questions, giving excuses and apologising.

- Speaks tentatively, with poor clarity and lots of repetition.
- Uses weak stage positions eg Upstage Left (USL).

Scene situations can be devised where an extremely high status character meets a very low status character and it may be interesting to observe who has the audience sympathy by the end of the scene. The clash between two high status characters can also be exciting and potentially dangerous (the leader may need to separate them if it escalates to physical violence!). Two extremely low status characters can also provide great comic outcomes.

Samuel Beckett's famous Absurdist play, *Waiting for Godot,* contains many scenes which explore status battles within relationships.

Warm-up—Are You Taking the…? {P, M, S}:

To bring the concept of status conflict to the forefront of the actors' minds, the following is a fun game to play in or out of mask. Two volunteers, one master, with a rolled-up newspaper or bopper, and one servant are required. The master improvises in front of the audience, speaking about the things they love most in the world, while the servant, standing behind the master, mocks everything the master does through mime, drawing the audience focus constantly. If the master turns around to look, the servant must quickly continue as if doing something else quite innocent. If this is not convincing or if the response is too slow, the master can hit servant with the bopper. Students love this game, especially if they get to be the master! Debrief afterwards: Where did the humour lie here? Where was the audience's focus? Who were you hoping would win?

Mistaken Apology {M, S}:

Two actors are required: one servant and one master. The servant is called to the master because they've done something wrong. The servant confesses to a multitude of wrongdoings, but not the deed their master had in mind. The master never gets the opportunity to address the original complaint because the servant is so busy apologising for everything else. This game works best at a quick pace. It's amusing to see what the master's reaction is to the other crimes.

Simple Scenarios In or Out of Mask {P, M, S}:

(a) Pantalone is getting ready for a hot date with Columbina who will arrive in five minutes. Unfortunately, there is a giant dog poo in the middle of the room. Pantalone calls for Arlecchino to get rid of the offending poo. Arlecchino tries to get out of the task. Who wins?

(b) Columbina wants Pantalone to give Arlecchino the weekend off so Arlecchino can take her to the movies. Pantalone has a long list of jobs for Arlecchino to do. What does Columbina do?
(c) Pulcinella has been ordered by Capitano to polish his medals. All Pulcinella wants to do is go to the races to watch his favourite horse run. What is the solution?
(d) Brighella has been assigned to Capitano as his valet for the weekend. Capitano is consistently cruel, assigning disgusting tasks to Brighella. Brighella knows that he will lose his job if there's trouble, even though he's strong enough to snap Capitano in half like a twig. Can Brighella come out on top?
(e) Dottore is in love with Columbina, his servant. Arlecchino is also Dottore's servant and is already going out with Columbina. Dottore wants to ask Columbina out on a date. Arlecchino wants to change Dottore's mind about Columbina; Dottore's amorous intentions are not easily swayed. Who ends up with Columbina?
(f) Make up your own simple master/servant scenario.

Countermask

As we have discussed earlier (p.87), countermask is where we get to see the other side of a character, or an actor playing 'against' the known attributes of a character. Countermask is commonly used in relation to status; it is usually revealed during moments of status reversal or during status transactions, such as when a character who is normally a master character assumes low status.

Take Capitano as an example. On one level, he is always bragging and pontificating about how tough and virile he is, but when challenged to a fight, we are surprised and delighted to find he's just a big wuss. While bragging, he is high status, when his true colours are revealed, his status plummets.

Brighella is another example. We know that he's a thug who is big and tough—this is what his mask suggests with his pugilist nose and beady eyes. However, Brighella is also capable of demonstrating great kindness, especially when someone such as Columbina melts his tough exterior. When he reveals his countermask, Brighella's status improves in our eyes—from low-life thug to endearing strongman. This takes real skill on the part of the actor and provides a depth to the character that transcends stereotype.

Every character has a countermask. The same is true for humans; once we stop treating people as stereotypes, our understanding, enjoyment and tolerance of them deepens. This is why a fat, lazy, stupid slob like Homer Simpson can be lovable at the same time—he loves his family and would do anything for them.

The following exercise can help students with the concept of countermask:

Bus Stop (inspired by Keith Johnstone) {M, S}:

Two Commedia characters (or non-Commedia if preferred) meet at a bus stop (or anywhere else) and begin with their known status. Try the combination of Dottore as master and Brighella as servant. Dottore is telling Brighella about all the surgical operations he has performed, but Brighella has a weak stomach. Instruct the students to have a status reversal occur about halfway through the impro. Brighella could vomit on Dottore who is allergic to diced carrots, or Brighella could be from the Board of Medical Practitioners and is there to serve Dottore with a summons to appear in court over a malpractice suit, or Brighella could have observed Dottore inappropriately touching one of his patients (Columbina) and is there to blackmail him. There are many possibilities. Go on to work with other scenarios and character combinations.

Nicky observed two actors in the bus stop exercise (with no preparation time) during rehearsals for *Stardust* (Chapter 7):

Michael (low status) and Kurt (high status), it was revealed, were two men who were strangers sitting on a park bench eating their lunch. As the improvised conversation progressed, the audience discovered Kurt was CEO of a large corporation and Michael was a cleaner in that same corporation. They displayed body language that reflected these roles. Their polite conversation became far more interesting when it was revealed that Michael was actually an undercover cop and had come across an incriminating piece of paper discarded in the CEO's bin that proved Kurt to be misappropriating company funds! The scene ended with Michael arresting Kurt. This type of status reversal (it would have been interesting to see Kurt regain his status by offering Michael a bribe!) is the stuff good Commedia is made of—the tension of relationships is palpable and the audience sees people outside of their normal circumstances.

Response Questions

After participating as audience or actors in any of the exercises in either the master/servant or countermask sections, answer the following questions:

1) *Was the status in your scene reversed or merely challenged? Why?*

2) *Were the actors successful in their use of countermask? That is, did the reversal provide more depth to character portrayal?*
3) *Did the actors' body language reflect the status of their characters?*
4) *Were the actors successful at manipulating tension in the relationships? Why/why not?*
5) *Was the scene funny? If so, where did the humour lie?*

Brighella (left) and Pulcinella (right) in *Stardust*
Illustrations by Benjamin Drake

MUSIC AND SINGING

Music and singing are an integral part of the fun of Commedia and particularly appropriate for Brighella and Arlecchino, although all characters can be part of musical sequences. Remember that it's not important to be able to sing beautifully—it's best to sing like the character speaks. Take any popular song and change the lyrics to suit. Here is an example from *Stardust* (Chapter 7):

BRIGHELLA:

Start spreading the glue,
Make a coffin today,
I'm gonna slice the Captain up,
Like pork, li-ike pork …

BURLE

Burle refers to verbal comedy, word play, puns and witticisms in Commedia. In successful Commedia, *burle* is beautifully balanced with the *lazzi* and physical comedy.

When playing Commedia, it is difficult for the novice to remember mask protocol, movement, voice and all the other aspects, as well as knowing what to say. The following activities are designed to help loosen the flow of dialogue necessary for an entertaining performance:

Warm-up—Word Association {LP, P, M, S}:

Students stand in a circle. When one person throws a tennis ball to another person in the group, they must say a word as they throw (e.g. 'chicken'). The person who catches the ball, then says a word which is associated with that word (e.g. 'drumstick') as they throw to another person, who throws the ball with a word related to 'drumstick' (e.g. 'cymbal'). This continues back and forth across the circle. Remind students that a good game is a fast game and there are no wrong answers. As actors get better at the game, you can add more balls in the circle as well as other challenges—for instance, you must clap before receiving the red ball, but not on the yellow ball.

Scene Without a Question {M, S}:

Three or four actors are asked to improvise a scene in a provided context with no preparation time. They are not allowed to ask any questions during the impro. The moment a person breaks this rule, they have to leave the stage immediately, leaving the other players to incorporate a reason why the person left as they continue the action. This activity forces students to think about what they are saying. They can play Commedia characters or other characters.

Actors could be provided with a few clues:

(a) Sample contexts:

- camping in the wilderness
- a clothes shop where there is a theft
- a wedding—the groom fails to show
- a birthday party—the cake is ruined

or

(b) Title ideas:

- The Great Burger Robbery
- The House That Jack Built

or

(c) Location, time, occupation:

- A butcher in a bakery at midnight
- A doctor in a bar at breakfast time

Misquoting Shakespeare {M, S}:

Many of Shakespeare's characters have been modelled on Commedia traditions. Students should experiment with these, and others. Misquoting Shakespeare especially suits doddery old men and stupid *zanni*.

Examples:

DOTTORE: Columbina, get thee to a distillery, no wait, a wet t-shirt competition, no wait, get thee into my four-poster bed…

or…

COLUMBINA: [*in a Bronx accent*] Yo Arlecchino, Arlecchino, wherefore is thy skinny butt…

Ask students to invent their own Shakespearean misquotations.

Modern Misquotations and References {P, M, S}:

CAPITANO: [*threateningly to Arlecchino in accent like Arnold Schwarzenegger*] I'll be back!

ARLECCHINO: Okay then, I'll be Mozart.

Try to list as many misquotes as possible, then assign them to different characters.

Finish the Sentence {P, M, S}:

This is a good game for getting students to understand Tartaglia's speech impediment; it also can apply to old men. For example, Tartaglia is awkwardly trying to tell Columbina how much he loves her, while Columbina is trying to helpfully avoid the topic:

TARTAGLIA: Did you know how much I love y-y-y-y-

COLUMBINA: Yak butter?

TARTAGLIA: No. [*Trying another tack*] I was wondering if you'd like to go to the m-m-m-m-m-m-

COLUMBINA: Mountains? No thanks, windy roads make me terribly car sick.

TARTAGLIA: No. [*Getting frustrated*] I just want you to put your hand on my d-d-d-

COLUMBINA: Digital clock? Sorry, but I don't know how to fix clocks when they're broken…

… and so on with Tartaglia becoming more and more frustrated and dejected.

Remember, in Commedia innuendo and vulgarity go hand in hand, so scenes featuring Tartaglia are ideal for exploring these qualities.

Getting Dottore's Dialogue Right {P, M, S}:

It is difficult to tackle Dottore's special brand of gobbledegook, especially during improvisation. Dottore's dialogue has a few features:

(a) Spoonerisms (swapping the first letter of two words around) e.g. 'the space of aids' instead of 'the ace of spades', or 'for real enjoyment give me a well-boiled icicle' [well-oiled bicycle].

(b) Misuse of clichés, e.g. 'A bird's bush is worth two in the hand', 'That's a catch 69 situation', 'Don't put all your eggs up one chicken'.

(c) Misuse of quotes (see above on misquoting Shakespeare).

(d) Tautologies (saying the same thing twice using different words) e.g. 'They arrived at the same time simultaneously'.

(e) Self-evident or obvious remarks e.g. 'When one is asleep it can be said that person is not awake'.

(f) Smatterings of made-up Latin words, e.g. When describing a pimple: 'It looks as if it could "del poppium splatium" on the mirror'; or completely made-up English words: 'It looks to me as if he's feeling a bit sqwellacious at the moment'.

(g) One word or topic reminds Dottore of something completely unrelated. An extreme example: 'I was examining a patient the other day when I noticed that he had a boil on his right gluteus. It's interesting that boil has two meanings—a boil meaning a sore, or the verb to boil, meaning cook. It reminded me of the time when I was treating patients in Ethiopia and I was boiling soup and I found a piece of parsley. Did you know that parsley comes from the Latin "parseo pasin" which means "to appear green"?'

(h) Attitude: All of Dottore's dialogue is delivered with such confidence and aplomb, while gesticulating knowledgeably on whatever topic is close to his heart, that one can't help but feel that even if what he says is absolute nonsense, there is a thread which somehow does make sense.

Have students find an obscure word in the dictionary, then create a lengthy meaning which includes a combination of made-up words and more obscure words. For a touch of irony, students could make up a meaning to the word *'sproloquio'* which is the traditional term for Dottore's perverse monologues! Have students rehearse, then present in Dottore's mask to an audience of 'university students', improvising without a script.

Response Questions

1) *Have you found dialogue difficult to invent for different characters? Which characters have you found most difficult? Why?*
2) *In your group of peers, who do you think is very successful at burle? What is it about their performance that makes them so successful?*
3) *The following misquotes are from* Stardust. *What Shakespeare play do they come from and how is the humour realised?*

CAPTAIN:

Now is the winter of our discontent,
Made glorious summer by this son of a gun,
And all the clouds that rained upon our island
In the deep bosom of a woman buried.

CAPTAIN:

Tomorrow and tomorrow and tomorrow
Creeps in this petty pace from day to day
To the last snail of recorded time.

SCENARIOS AND PUTTING IT ALL TOGETHER

KISS (Keep It Short and Simple)

Our Commedia apprentices should now have arrived at the synthesising phase of their learning. The apprentice Italian chef needs to master simple recipes so that not too much time, energy or ingredients are wasted, and confidence grows. The same is true for apprentice theatre makers. Initially, when devising their own scenarios, they should keep them simple, with only a few characters. In this way, students have the opportunity to fully explore the characters' obsessions. For example, Flavio is late for a secret meeting with Isabella—he's been out saving the forests. Isabella grows impatient. Flavio finally arrives, full of apologies and lover's sighs. They begin to argue about who loves the other more.

The Letter {M, S}:

A letter is often a good place to begin a scenario if apprentices are stuck for ideas. Someone receives a letter at the beginning of the scene which dictates what happens for the remainder. Try not to give too much away at once—that way actors will invite the curiosity of the audience.

For instance, Pantalone receives a letter from his financial advisors saying that his company has been placed into receivership. The scene may simply start with Pantalone responding to the letter by fainting or going into apoplexy. As Arlecchino (or other *zanni*) revives him, his dialogue is barely comprehensible: 'No, they can't, they simply can't …Oh dear, I see pigs flying…' Arlecchino eventually extracts the truth from him, then offers illogical suggestions for saving his company before accidentally arriving at a solution that Pantalone jumps at. The first suggestion could be: 'Why don't you pretend you're not home?'; the second suggestion: 'Why don't you sell your fake Monet painting?'; then the third suggestion, the solution: 'Why don't you put on a wig and fly to Greece and let the shareholders pick up the tab?'

A more complex scenario {M, S}:

During a longer rehearsal time or longer lesson, have apprentices create a scenario in groups of four or five which contains the following essential ingredients:

The cast must contain at least:

- Two masters
- Two servants
- One captain
- Two lovers

(Some actors will need to play two roles.)

There must be at least several of the following actions and events within the scenario:

- Theft
- Chase
- Fight
- Disguise
- *Lazzi* and *burle*
- Secret meeting
- Dark/night scene

The above events may occur in any sequence or a few at the same time (e.g. a chase and a fight in a dark room, or a secret meeting at night in disguise).

Try adding other ingredients such as romance, revenge, countermask, status reversal, etc.

The scenario can finish with:

- A resolution with a song/dance (e.g. *Love is in the Air* or *Rich Man's World*), or well-known tunes with new lyrics, or original tunes with original lyrics.

- A freeze frame (tableau).
- The characters make their exit.

(If a curtain call is taken, it should be done in character with masks on.)

Students may work without masks until their *canovacci* is worked out and they have physically explored the characters and sequences in their scenarios.

Debrief: After all the groups have presented their scenarios each student is asked what things worked best for the audience and what things the actor most enjoyed about being in the performance. Finally, the discussion can move to things to avoid or be careful of in future performances as well as ways to improve future work on Commedia dell'arte.

Extended Commedia Role Play—Murder in the Marketplace {P, M, S}:

Once apprentices are accomplished at handling Commedia scenarios and their typical complications, an enjoyable game which extends their characterisation and improvisation skills is Murder in the Marketplace. This is an extremely popular game with all students and one in which they really begin to own their learning.

Step 1—Context:

The setting is a typical market (e.g. fruit and vegetable, trash and treasure, flea market) with all Commedia characters cast before the game begins. Divide the class into half audience, half participants. If you have enough masks, it is interesting to watch multiples of some characters interact with one another—three Pantalones could create quite a stir! Have all students involved in the game close their eyes and lower their heads while the leader chooses a murderer by tapping one person on the shoulder three times.

Rules:

(a) The way the murderer kills is to say the word 'death' in a sentence to somebody, eg. 'What a lovely death necklace you are wearing'.

(b) Anybody at all who overhears the word 'death', other than the intended victim, must also die.

(c) The victim then has to talk to three more people before dying and, of course, they have to die as dramatically as possible before dragging themselves off to the 'graveyard', which means they are out of the game. They may not speak to anyone else once this occurs.

(d) Only the murderer can say 'death'. The murderer cannot shout it out to everybody—this would sabotage the game.

Step 2—Playing the Game:

(a) The game begins after stall holders are selected and shops are set up in the space.
(b) All characters are in role either as stall owners or customers. The murderer can either be a stall owner or a customer.
(c) If one of the participants thinks they know who the murderer is, they approach the leader with an accusation. The leader stops the action, announces the accusation, and asks if there's anybody else who will second the accusation. If there's nobody, the action resumes.
(d) If there is someone to second the accusation, and the seconder is correct, the murderer dies and the game is over. If the seconder is incorrect, then the seconder dies and play resumes.

Step 3—Debriefing the Game:

Once the game is over, ask audience members for feedback for the players:
(a) What did you think of characterisation?
(b) How well did the players sustain their roles?
(c) Did they act in accordance with their attributes?
(d) What did you think of their interactions?
Once they have played this game a few times, students can feel free to change location to suit themselves (eg. Murder in the Nightclub, Murder in the Supermarket).

Murderous Secrets {S}:

There are many other variations to Murder in the Marketplace, some a little more involved. Give each of the characters an objective and a secret. You could have actors make these up for themselves or you could provide them. For example, Columbina's objective is to try and get a raise in wages from Pantalone, and her secret is that she told Dottore she would marry him, but that she doesn't want her boyfriend Arlecchino to know.

or

The objective and secret could be a little more ridiculous. For example, Brighella's objective is to collect rent from all the stall holders, but his secret is that he's been attending anger management classes and he has been instructed not to hurt anybody.

or

The objective and secret could be completely absurd. For example, Arlecchino's objective is to collect one hair from everybody's head for an experiment the Doctor is conducting, but his secret is that anybody who coughs makes him want to juggle.

It is important that students do not divulge either their objective or their secret before the game begins. This game is as much fun for observers as participants and debriefing afterwards should prove lively.

Response Questions

1) *Which character do you like playing most? Why do you think this is so?*
2) *Which character do you like playing least? Why is this so?*
3) *What area/s do you still think you need to improve upon before tackling public performance?*
4) *What excites you most about playing Commedia? Why?*
5) *What excites you least about playing Commedia? Why?*

Capitano in *Stardust*
Illustration by Benjamin Drake

COMMEDIA OZ – Putting It All Together {S}

Inventing Commedia scenarios in a modern Australian context ensures loads of possibilities. There is an abundance of topics to choose from—the Australian temperament is famously unselfconscious and as we don't mind making fools of ourselves from time to time, this creates endless opportunities for satire. Originality should be encouraged wherever possible. As an audience member, there are few things more painful to watch than an unimaginative Commedia performance that plays the same old clichéd, tired jokes of yesteryear.

Laughter comes when audiences identify with the subject matter and recognise things from their own lives. For instance, historically Pantalone's costume had a money pouch secured around his waist that looked like a scrotum, so jokes about his nether regions always ensued. Modern audiences may find this a little obscure as fashions have changed, so why not update the image? Give Pantalone a 'manbag', American Express Gold Card or, better still, Telstra shares! The secret is to modernise and place everything in a contemporary setting. Satirical comment and pointed jokes are sure to find their audience.

So, how to go about creating your own original Commedia recipe?

Context:

A good place to start is by deciding on the context of your show. Look for something with political underpinnings:

- Globalisation
- Telecommunications wars
- Refugees
- Terrorism
- Politicians (Pantalone could represent numerous politicians—those eyebrows are a real giveaway!)
- Environmental disasters—uranium mining, shopping malls, Gold Coast development, water shortages, corrupt land deals
- Morals, values, social mores, religious beliefs
- Trade unions, sporting clubs, community associations

Checklist toward a successful performance:

Once the context is chosen, apprentices may find the following guide useful when working through performance tasks. This guide is a mixture of Goldoni and Gozzi methods—some parts are improvised, others are written. Tick off each step as it is completed.

- Choose characters and establish roles and relationships. Some questions to ponder:
  (a) What role/s are we good at? Who do we want to play?
  (b) Do these preferences for roles allow for enough balance? Are there enough masters vs. servants, goodies vs. baddies, lovers' trysts, etc.?
  (c) Will the group need to double up on roles? Does one actor need to play more than one part?
- Write a brief outline of your story (scenario)—fifty words or less.
  For example, rich Pantalone, a land developer, loves Dottore's daughter (*inamorata*) who is in love with *inamorato*, local geologist and do-gooder. Servants intercept and intervene. Happy ending.
- Break it into scenes:
  1. Pantalone talks about the wedding to *inamorata* and issues orders to Arlecchino.

2. The lovers meet. etc.

- Improvise this story for a while with your cast. Is it working?
- Add at least one *lazzo.*
- Include *burle*—some jokes and witty banter should begin to emerge at this stage and help shape the scenes.
- Choose several from the following list to have in your show:

  Theft—could be money, a heart, jewels, a will, a key, a map.

  Chase—never have the stage empty. Could be a distraction: 'Look over there!'

  Disguise—should be obvious to the audience. Can use disguise to become another person or object such as a piece of furniture.

  Dark/night scene—done in full light for the audience. The actors sneak up, bumping into one another as if they can't see.

  Secret meeting—between lovers, baddies, goodies, a ghost.

  Resolution with a song/dance—could be modern. Choose a modern song or a traditional song, changing its lyrics. It should sum up what the circumstances are at the end of the show and the characters' final status positions.

  End in a freeze frame (tableau)—this is traditional so that people passing by could see what happened during the show and would become interested in attending next time. Lovers are reunited, servants are happy, masters thwarted and hopefully someone got the money!

  Feel free to add anything else you've invented!
- Commit yourselves to writing a numbered list of scenes (*canovacci*) that can be used backstage as a guide. Using *Stardust* as an example:

  1. A Stardust welcome.
  2. Pantalone pushes progress.
  3. Pantalone plays with the 'guests', etc.
- Keep a record of what is said (the good stuff, anyway) so that the story begins to take a more polished shape.
- How are your movements? Is your voice reflective of character? Are you working with appropriate physicality? Is there enough energy?
- Costuming—what choices are you making to Australian-ise your character/s? Check with one another how you are going to do this so that your choices are consistent. Keep choices simple, especially for quick character changes.

- Props—who's keeping track of props? Make a list. Use essential props only. Perhaps one broom handle can be used in different ways—a walking stick, sword, hobby horse and gun.
- Practise, polish, practise, polish, present.

Post-Performance Response Questions

1) *Did you have fun? Why or why not?*
2) *How did you feel during the performance?*
3) *How did you feel after the performance?*
4) *(i) Choose one example of dramatic tension in your performance.*
   (ii) Explain how your cast manipulated the tension.
   (iii) How was the tension resolved? Was it effective?
5) *Do you think the overall mood of the group's performance was successful?*
6) *In what ways could you improve your show?*
7) *Do you have a favourite moment in the show? Why was it your favourite?*

CHAPTER 6

Lecoq au Vin: Jacques Lecoq

TRAINING ACTORS

Jacques Lecoq introduced a truly original approach to the training of actors and the development of theatrical performance during his long career as a theatre practitioner, teacher and theorist. Born in Paris in 1921, Lecoq taught until the day before his death on 19 January 1999.

Lecoq has been an inspiration to untold numbers of actors, dancers, puppeteers, writers, designers, clowns, musicians, directors and teachers from around the world. There can be no reference to the modern exploration of Commedia dell'arte without recognition of his influence.

Lecoq believed that while England gave the world the great theatre of Elizabethan times, continental Europe also made two great contributions—Greek Tragedy and the Commedia dell'arte.

In 1991, at 70 years of age, Jacques Lecoq made his first and only visit to Australia to conduct masterclasses at the International Workshop Festival, Adelaide. What follows is the substance of an interview conducted with Lecoq for the national youth arts journal, *Lowdown* (June 1991) through interpreter Faye Lecoq, his wife and manager of the school.

Steven Gration (SG): How did you begin your career in theatre?

Jacques Lecoq (JL): I began my career in the fields of architecture and physiotherapy. As a teacher of architecture in Paris I became fascinated by discoveries in the dynamics of movement that brings life to space. My relationship to sport through physiotherapy brought me to an understanding of human movement and its possibilities.

I began my theatrical career in 1945 as an actor and during my early days as a performer I was invited to work as a choreographer-director at the University of

Padua and later with the Greek Theatre in Syracuse [Italy]. I began to develop an approach to mime or movement, which perhaps had some echoes of the great Jacques Copeau.

Copeau (1879–1949) was a French director, writer, designer, critic, teacher and theorist who revolutionised European theatre and developed physical theatre techniques in the early part of the twentieth century as a reaction against Realism.

Lecoq teamed up with painter Dario Fo and sculptor Amleto Sartori while in Italy (1948–56) and, with them, developed some of his teaching approaches which are still used today. Working with Piccolo Teatro di Milano, Lecoq convinced Sartori to research and reintroduce the Rennaissance art of making masks from leather rather than papier mâché, which was popular at the time. This technique of sculpting leather masks, combined with Lecoq's approach to physical performance, contributed to the revival of the Commedia form two hundred years after its demise in Italy. Master mask-maker Sartori passed on his skills to his son, Donato Sartori, who in turn trained another Italian from Florence, Paolo Consiglio, in the art of mask-making in the Commedia tradition. Consiglio regularly visits Australia to conduct leather mask-making workshops.

Further explorations by Lecoq with Sartori, Fo, Giorgio Strehler and Paolo Grassi led to a deeper understanding of Greek Tragedy and Chorus, Commedia, melodrama, clowns, *bouffon* and mask, particularly Neutral Mask. Lecoq returned to Paris and opened his theatre school, the L'École Internationale de Théâtre Jacques Lecoq, in 1956.

SG: What is the structure of training at your school and what type of student does it attract?

JL: It is a two-year course and students have come from seventy-five different countries. I prefer the students to be at least twenty-three to twenty-four years old, with some life experience, who wish to be involved professionally in theatre as actor, director and author. It is not a course for those who just want to learn to 'express themselves'. The students are all on probation for the first three months.

First year begins in Silence and the Neutral Mask. My work has at times been misinterpreted. Mime is not the aim of the school but the motor that drives it. I am not a 'mime' teacher in the way we know mime through performers such as Marcel Marceau. Mime as it was interpreted many years ago is finished. In the past mimes walked on the spot without knowing where they were going. Today a mime is an actor who moves better than an actor. Mimes are capable of physically interpreting anything they see, read or hear. Mime is a theatre of gesture and image.

Students get rid of mannerisms and tricks they have developed from their culture or formal training. Through movement they explore plants and animals, the elements, material matter and colours. Students make their own mask—any kind of mask—and this leads to interpreting character and enlarging their way of acting. They improvise with their characters and then use my specially developed Expressive Masks. Theatre is a game.

Students are asked to 'act a character', not the psycho-drama of themselves. They study how human nature works; they go to different places to observe how life works. They visit railway stations, the markets, the streets. Human nature is explored through the passions or states of being. Laughter, crying, jealousy and flattery are examined.

In the 1990s Lecoq was particularly interested in jealousy, or 'Why not me?', as a source for theatrical exploration.

Each day the students work on their own in groups of five to seven for an hour and a half preparing a performance on a theme we suggest which is as simple as 'A Place, An Event'. The work is presented to the whole school at the end of each week. I call these sessions 'auto-cours'.

After an understanding of the dynamics of human passion is gained, students develop approaches to forms of art such as painting, architecture, poetry and music through the human body. Miming a poem and abstractions of gesture could lead to beautiful translations of poetry. To translate T.S. Eliot into French is impossible—it loses its dynamic sense. The essential thing in poetry is what is not said, what is between the words, and this movement is an effective way of translating and interpreting a poem.

Towards the end of first year the students study different styles of theatre and the traditional forms are pushed into Commedia or melodrama from everyday life or events.

The second year at the school (for the one in three students who are invited to stay on) explores different dramatic territories using the foundations of the first year.

SG: What are the essential elements of the second year of training at your school?

JL: Students explore what makes the public cry or laugh and where we find the spirit of justice or morality. Approaching the 'Great Sentiments', students explore the seven deadly sins—lust, greed, gluttony, envy, etc. —through melodrama.

Immediately following this exploration, everything is mocked through the world of the Bouffon. Students approach the mystery of the folly and madness of the Bouffon, who are crazy but, as fools, reveal the truth. The Bouffon takes students back to childhood. Who understands children? Their mothers perhaps, but I doubt it. Children are mysteries, they are crazy. Bouffon leads students into explorations of the devil in us all. While amusing us the Bouffon also reaches tragic dimensions. This leads students into Tragedy, the Greek Chorus and the Hero. Students express these elements through events that are important to them or current events such as the Iraqi War. [*Lecoq was referring to the first Gulf war in 1990–91.*]

Finally students come full circle to the Commedia dell'arte, the human comedy. Since the 1960s I have also taken the Commedia into Clown studies. We all own a personal clown and we are all clowns because clowns all fail somewhere. Students then find an approach to a text, blending and mixing all they have learnt over the two years. The authors of the texts change each year but they have included Shakespeare, Chekhov and Molière. At the end of second year I give each student a 'personal command', a theme for them to create a dramatic product of about seven minutes in length that is extremely personal. This also becomes the seedling for future shows with professional companies. For some students the command is taken on as a lifetime pursuit through the theatre companies they found or work with and the events they create. An example of a command might be 'Tomorrow daylight will come'.

In his text, *The Moving Body, Teaching Creative Theatre*, Lecoq describes the second part of training as preparing the students for an 'exploration of a full range of dramatic territories, their relations to one another… based on five principal territories which generate others'. (2001) The principles are:

Melodrama (Grand Emotions)
Commedia dell'arte (Human Comedy)
Bouffons (from Grotesque to Mystery)
Tragedy (Chorus and Hero)
Clowns (Burlesque and Absurd)

SG: How successful is the training, do you think?

JL: Normally people who have completed two years at the school find professional theatre work. Occasionally they might marry, settle down or become a priest or a painter! A straight line doesn't exist in life; it's like a game of billiards. It's like wine. A good wine should not be drunk immediately. Even if the students work in television or uninteresting theatre companies, the two years training will assist them. After working for five to ten years in theatre some students return for a third year to train as teachers—a very pedagogical way of teaching, very structured.

SG: A number of Australians have studied with you over the years and they have had a strong influence on theatre in Australia. Have you observed anything unique about the Australian students?

JL: Australians have a big sense of space when they move, and also Texans.

Director George Ogilvie was one of the first Australians to study with Lecoq. Ogilvie's work in theatre, television and film is undeniably powerful and inventive. His co-direction on the film *Mad Max: Beyond Thunderdome* (1984) saw the plot littered with clowns, *bouffon*, Commedia characters and tragic heroes who were true to Lecoq's theories and practices. Another Lecoq graduate, Geoffrey Rush, was renowned for his physical and engaging performances in theatre before being cast in the role of David Helfgott in the film *Shine* for which he won both Academy and Golden Globe Awards for Best Actor in 1997.

Other Australians to have studied with Lecoq include Isabelle Anderson of Queensland who is now based in New York as a teacher, director and performer of Shakespeare's plays; John Bolton who established a highly reputable acting school in Melbourne; Russell Dykstra who won an Australian Film Institute Best Actor Award in 1999 for his role in the film *Soft Fruit* and has since gone on to further success in theatre, television and film roles; Dr Judith Pippen, Dominique Sweeney, Michael Newbold, Will Hodgson, Therese Collie, Russell Fewster, Marie Dupont and Alex Pinder. These artists have worked consistently in the fields of theatre, film, television or as researchers and teachers in universities and schools, since returning from their studies with Lecoq. They have also been responsible for creating many original theatrical performances in Australia and utilising their Lecoq experiences to train actors.

There are numerous other examples of Australian graduates of the Lecoq School working with Australian and international companies such as *Cirque du Soleil*, Théâtre du Complicité, Théâtre du Soleil, Footsbarn Travelling Theatre, Mummenschanz and Commedia troupes throughout the world, too many in fact to mention here.

SG: What is it we don't know about the Commedia dell'arte that we can't necessarily get from books?

JL: Copeau tried to identify the spirit of the Commedia in French everyday life. Meyerhold tried to do that too in his work.

Vsevolod Meyerhold (1874–1942) was a Soviet actor and director who emerged as a leading exponent of Experimental Drama after joining the Moscow Art Theatre in 1918. He developed a system of training actors called 'Bio-mechanics' but fell out with Stanislavski over his criticism of Realism as a style of performance.

Other French artists who were interested in Mask performance were Etienne Decroux, Antonin Artaud and Jean-Louis Barrault. I am probably closer to Barrault than Decroux in the form of theatre I teach. But I have collected every book ever printed on the Commedia since the 1600s, yet I still continue to research and make new discoveries about the Commedia. There is always something missing when reading these books because no book has ever been entirely written from an actor's perspective.

The books are written from an observer's perspective and so actors should feel a freedom to find how the Commedia relates to them in performance. Actors are constantly discovering and rediscovering during their explorations of the Commedia and it can be readily transposed into modern times and events.

Likewise, with Greek Tragedy we know very little about the details of how it was performed. The music in Greek Tragedies is unknown but they were musical.

I suspect they were like a musical tragic review with singing, dancing and drama... What is left is only a skeleton of the text. I am fascinated by the use of Chorus—that fifteen people on stage together is not funny, it is not Comedy, it creates Tragedy. Greek Chorus is ancient but also modern.

Lecoq sees Greek Tragedy and Chorus as a foundation for the actor to build on. His students explore spatial awareness in groups, group 'architecture', the use of physical and gestural language, the language of Mask, the relationship of the Hero to the Chorus and so on. Later in training, these are linked to the nature of the Commedia dell'arte (see Chapter 1).

One student from Argentina developed a Chorus event related to the mothers of 'The Missing' in the political context of South America. It was a Modern Tragedy.

SG: Do you think Shakespeare may have been influenced by Commedia troupes visiting Britain?

JL: Being French I do not have a great knowledge of Shakespeare but I believe he may have been heavily influenced by the Italian actors who travelled through Europe and England. It is only in recent times that companies have decided that Shakespeare should be a talking heads event rather than the highly physical performances of Shakespeare's time. But I see the spirit of the Commedia in everyday modern life and it is as relevant today as it was three hundred years ago.

During Lecoq's 1991 workshops at the Adelaide International Festival he worked with thirty Australian participants over seven days. He proved adept at working with such a large number of students as he covered some of the main principles of his teaching in Paris. He has always maintained that his teaching is a time for students to rediscover the elements of nature they have forgotten, and how they correspond to the intimate moments of human emotion. In the workshops, students explored Gestural Language, Neutral Mask, and Commedia dell'arte through the 'expression of the actor as author and the body as performer'. Lecoq's focus was on the body in action and the quality of the human being to mime the world in order to know it. He has made it possible to break the bonds of traditional silent mime to give way to a theatre where gesture and image are equally important.

My fascination with Lecoq's teachings was enhanced by my observations of this European master's childlike curiosity. He told me at the end of our interview that while he was in Australia he had an 'appointment' with the Southern Cross star constellation. He was like an excited child waiting for a Christmas present when I offered to point out the Southern Cross to him in the Adelaide night sky. My rough drawing to complement his personal sighting of the Cross was treasured by him as though it were a work of art. Lecoq was also fascinated by South Australian wines. He documented every wine he tasted by lifting the label off the bottle and placing it in his journal. If a label wouldn't lift off he wrote down details from the label to add to his collection of wine memories. He believed his students must go away and allow their work to mature over a period of years and 'like a good bottle of wine, get better with age'.

Lecoq's theatre and training methods are now documented in an excellent book, *The Moving Body, Teaching Creative Theatre* (2001). Lecoq can also be observed teaching at his school in the documentary film, *Les Deux Voyages* (1999). Since his death in 1999, Jacques Lecoq's school has continued to train remarkable artists from around the world under the direction of his wife, Faye Lecoq. Students are instructed by graduates of the school who have completed a third year of pedagogical training, as well as internationally recognised industry professionals.

Response Questions

1) *Who else has had an influence on the physical training of actors in Australia and/or overseas?*
2) *What cultures (other than Western culture) train performers in physical skills?*
3) *What are the types of performances or names of the styles of performances these cultures produce?*
4) *Which companies or individual artists from these cultures have had a strong influence on local or world theatre?*

CHAPTER 7

Bon Appetito! A Contemporary Australian Commedia dell'arte Script

STARDUST by Steven Gration

WRITER-DIRECTOR'S FOREWORD

This foreword is to give teachers, students and actors an insight into how *Stardust* was cooked up. The ingredients which were most important in its creation involved the following approach to auditioning, writing, devising, rehearsing and performing the play.

The Teaching Artist

I assume that the director of a live theatrical production is a teaching artist rather than merely a 'product manager'. The latter evokes images of a police officer directing traffic on stage to a predetermined plan of action. If I wanted to be a traffic cop I would have joined the police force.

A director does much more than direct traffic on a stage. They must be responsible for teaching their cast about relevant theatre history, cultural contexts and the specifics of the work they are creating. In addition, they need to place themselves in a position from which they can view the production through the eyes of the intended audience.

Directors need to be eclectic in their interests in theatre forms and styles, and to have a wide knowledge of a variety of cultural expressions—Australian directors, for instance, should be knowledgeable of non-Anglo cultural traditions. The director should also be curious about people from all walks of life, reading about them and engaging in conversation with them, when possible, in an effort to appreciate ideas and perceptions from anywhere in the world.

This parallels the path of the effective teacher who attempts to cater for individual difference in the classroom. Teachers encounter fewer behavioural problems when they allow for the fact that not every child learns in the same way or at the same rate. Nor do individuals perceive or interpret events in the same way due to differences in the cultural, social, economic and political influences in their lives, as well as physical differences. As teachers, we can set up an atmosphere or environment where people want to learn. This philosophy is central not only to our work in teaching, but also as directors, in the way we relate to actors and audiences.

Our work as a director should always endeavour to celebrate the individual actor's skills and experiences. These then feed into the strength of the ensemble of artists on any project, be it a self-devised work, new text or established script. Building an ensemble atmosphere should be the aim of every project, whether it be for an audition process, a cast of project actors who may never work together again, or a collective of artists who remain together for many months or even years.

Many directors 'block' the play (scripted or self-devised) during the first week of rehearsal then do endless runs of the performance. The blocking process involves the director telling the actors where and when to stand, move and speak. These directors then wonder why opening night lacks life and energy! And that's blocking at its best! At its worst is when the costumes and set arrive at rehearsal and all the blocking has to be redone because it doesn't work on stage with the real objects. It's ironic that in the art of improvisation, the term 'to block' means to obstruct or ignore opportunities and offers between performers. Rehearsals need to be kept open and interesting and it is far better to allow actors to 'discover' and 'own' their performances than to simply run scenes over and over.

I can't imagine anything more frustrating for an actor than to walk away from four weeks of rehearsal and go into a performance season with nothing but a 'blocking' pattern imposed by the director. They will have gained very little that is useful for their future development.

Auditions

The theatre industry seems obsessed with 'cattle call' auditions but very few actors enjoy them. The cattle call generally requires an actor to sit outside a studio or room with several others who are going for the same role. One at a time the actors are invited into the inner sanctum to perform a couple of monologues in front of a director and sometimes a panel of two or three others. These 'others' sit behind a desk judging the actor's performance. Everyone is uncomfortable including the panel who can often appear intimidating to the auditonees.

The monologues tend to be prescribed by the director or theatre company and frequently involve a piece from a classical play (usually Shakespeare) and a well-known contemporary play. Some lazy actors prefer this type of audition because they don't have to learn anything new and can trot out the same old pieces time after time. If the audition is for a specific role in a play, the actor may be asked to perform an excerpt from that character's dialogue in the play. This is called a 'cold read' and usually leaves the onlookers cold if the person auditioning is a poor reader. Most actors I have spoken to don't believe they can show their best work in a cattle call audition. Most actors perform as part of an ensemble so why set up solo auditions that do not reflect the working situation?

As a director I prefer to conduct 'workshop auditions' in which several actors work together for up to two hours on warm-ups, improvisation, text and ensemble techniques. This gives them an opportunity to experience my working process and to gain an insight into whether or not they would like to work with me. They are assessing me just as much as I am assessing them. At the conclusion of the workshop audition, actors often say that even if they don't get the role they have had an enjoyable time and learnt much from the process.

The *Stardust* Audition

I needed a cast of three actors to play multiple roles in *Stardust* as the intention was to tour the show to secondary schools in Queensland. Although the play would have up to nine characters, the actors were professionals and the producer, Commotion Theatre Company, had a budget for only three actors' wages.

In addition to directing, I would be developing the *Stardust* script through improvisation by the actors. Starting with a list of scene descriptions (*canovacci*), a list of characters and locations, the actors I employed would have to be capable of improvising sections of the play so that we could work up a script. They also needed to be skilled at improvising during performances and interacting with the audience.

I conducted a workshop audition with eight actors over a two-hour period. I was looking for performers who had strong vocal and physical skills, wild imaginations and could improvise generously with other actors. They needed to work well in an ensemble atmosphere and respond positively to the mask performance techniques I was to reveal to them. I was also looking for actors who were curious about the traditions and contemporary possibilities of the Commedia dell'arte style.

At the beginning of the *Stardust* workshop audition, I asked the actors to do a personal warm-up and, while appearing to be doing paperwork, I discreetly observed their work. I wanted to see which actors were capable of self-supervision, self-motivation and had a warm-up regime that was appropriate for an actor committed to their craft.

I then conducted a rigorous physical and vocal warm-up during which I noted those actors who could handle the demands of the exercises, but also those brave actors who may not have worked in such a way before but were willing to try! We covered basic tumbling, handstands, lifts and counter balances, explored a variety of vocal sounds involving the mimicking of animals, and the singing of children's songs and rounds to explore harmonies.

I set up improvisations and ensemble-building games where teamwork was important. I gave each actor a solo task, in which they had five to ten minutes to devise and rehearse a small amount of text to present to their fellow auditionees as a short performance. The audition process became a sharing of ideas and offerings rather than a secret event at which those auditioning never get to see what other actors can do.

I have known actors who met other actors for the first time at a workshop audition. After witnessing, first hand, the skills on offer at the audition, they have later teamed up to work together in creating their own performances. The opportunity to find creative partnerships is a by-product of the workshop audition process and can offset the disappointment of not getting the part in a play or the job with an ensemble.

If I had conducted the usual 'cattle call' audition, spending approximately fifteen minutes with each actor, it would have taken the same amount of time as the workshop audition, but proven far less effective. The workshop format allowed me to witness a wide variety of skills, personalities and the participants' potential to work in a collaborative and cooperative manner.

The specific Commedia nature of *Stardust* demanded that the actors be open to a highly physical style, utilising mask performance techniques and developing contact and rapport with an audience. The auditionees watched each other present their solo work and, later, group performances based on Commedia scenarios that I had given them. This allowed me to gauge how comfortable they were in taking risks through the way they interacted and connected with the audience—a very important element in the Commedia dell'arte style.

During the audition I conducted two different mask techniques, Aussie Physical Approach (see p.75) and Johnstone's Mask Trance (see p.78), which are described in detail in Chapter 4. The selection of the *Stardust* cast was difficult as all the actors had strong skills and an affinity with masks and the audience, so I asked the auditionees to each fill in a chart listing their other skills and interests. These skills proved invaluable in the creation of the Commedia performance style in *Stardust*.

The skills and interest chart covered the following areas:

Music, singing.

Martial arts, circus, gymnastics.

Technical (sound, lighting, sewing, design, construction, etc.)

Dance/movement training
Other languages, including deaf-sign
Cultural influences (e.g. caber throwing, Italian cooking, university debating)
Miscellaneous (e.g. skate boarding, mountaineering, lifesaving)

I am always amazed at the richness of the life experiences and backgrounds that artists bring with them to an audition or rehearsal room and which have the potential to enhance their performance work.

I chose my three actors for *Stardust* based on all the above-mentioned exercises. Kurt, Mary and Michael were multi-skilled, responded positively to the mask techniques and worked well in ensemble games requiring teamwork. They were also willing to go beyond mundane Realism and to take risks when improvising and interacting with the audience.

The other auditionees were strong in many areas but a few would occasionally sink back into Realism in their physical interactions with each other and the audience. Some could play female roles with strength, but couldn't make the transition to playing male roles with the same focus and commitment. My *Stardust* cast would each need to play several characters, some crossing gender boundaries.

After offering the three actors employment in the project we found out that the touring schedule might clash with some of Michael's prior commitments. I didn't want to lose him completely so I tried to be flexible by offering another actor, Nicky, the possibility of understudying Michael's roles. Nicky had auditioned brilliantly and took to the mask work like a dolphin to water. She also had a unique ability, as a female performer, to play male roles with strength and humour. Unfortunately she wasn't available for the whole season of *Stardust* but agreed to understudy Michael and be a part of the rehearsal process. We had a 'win win' situation with Michael able to stay in the project and Nicky performing his roles when he wasn't available.

When I sat down and wrote up the skills that Michael, Kurt, Mary and Nicky had between them I was amazed at what else they could do. The list included acrobatics, guitar, singing, juggling, German language, percussion, keyboard and ballet—just to name a few. I was determined to use some of these skills in *Stardust*. There would definitely be music, singing, dance, circus and other languages in the production!

Stardust Rehearsals

The rehearsal process built on the foundations of the audition process. This would include the continuation of warm-ups, along with physical and vocal training. We immersed ourselves in serious physical and vocal warm-up exercises to develop strength, stamina and flexibility in these areas. The actors also offered us warm-up ideas and exercises they had learnt from previous productions or classes.

We developed and expanded circus routines such as juggling and tumbling, balances, lifts, slapstick and stage fighting techniques. We became used to each other's body weight, strength, flexibility and 'handling' one another. There is no room for embarrassment about touching other actors in the Commedia style!

I gave the actors scenarios or script ideas for them to improvise around as a means of solving solo and group performance problems, often utilising mask techniques. At other times I asked them to develop comic business between characters or with objects such as a bag of money, a wooden cooking spoon or a rubber chicken. Often these improvisations ended up in the script.

Training

I believe directors have a responsibility for the development of not only the artists with whom they are working, but of theatre itself as an art form. If we open up choices for actors then we open up the potential to develop a broad and deep theatrical language which we can then share amongst ourselves, as well as other artists and our audiences. So, every rehearsal period of mine has skills development built into it. I run classes and workshops in my areas of strength and engage specialists in fields such as a stage-fighting or choreography when appropriate.

The process of training, skills development, the use of children's games, improvisation, approach to text, physical/vocal classes, and the exploration of different styles and forms applies whether I am working with children, community members, adult amateurs or professional actors. I incorporate this process whether it is for a weekly class, a four-week full-time or a three-month part-time rehearsal period. The training and development activities are chosen to affirm and challenge the actors at levels that do not overwhelm or inhibit them. It is my aim that each actor finishes a project with more skills and insight than they possessed at the outset.

Improvisation

A major element in rehearsals when devising original material, rehearsing a new script or an established text, is the practice of improvising. Interpretative possibilities are opened up through improvisational frameworks and the ensemble atmosphere this develops. The principles of improvisation involve the understanding of concepts such as Offer, Accept, Block, Risk, Yield, Endow, Extend, Advance, Transition, Status and Protect (see Glossary).

Training in improvisation gives actors the opportunity to understand how drama is structured, how dialogue is developed and how status affects physicality and character interactions in both comedy and tragedy.

Theatre History

In any rehearsal context, actors need to develop a common theatrical language. I run Theatre History workshops where the actors do practical devising and performance exercises in different theatre genres. I cover major territories such as Greek Comedy and Tragedy, Commedia dell'arte (even if we aren't doing a Commedia performance), Elizabethan, Restoration or Royal Court Theatre, Epic Theatre, Absurdist Theatre and Theatre of Cruelty. This gives the actors a wider choice in creating their characters and a broader knowledge of staging possibilities. In addition, if, as director, I suggest that 'this scene is a Greek Chorus event' or 'this moment is an Absurdist one', we all know what I am talking about. We can then translate it into a physical exploration of the style or genre in rehearsal and if it works we can use it in the actual performance.

Mask Techniques

Each day the *Stardust* actors spent time practising the Mask Techniques detailed in Chapter 4 (Aussie Physical Approach p.75 and Johnstone's Mask Trance p.78) until they were adept at assisting one another with the different approaches to mask character work.

Devising and Writing *Stardust*

We continued training and devising material as described above for the first two weeks of our six-week part-time rehearsal period, which consisted of four-hour periods, five times a week. During weeks three and four we found ways to apply the exercises, improvisations and mask techniques to the characters and scenes I had written for *Stardust.* These scenes were written outside rehearsal times and were heavily influenced by the work of the actors during the previous rehearsal. When new script material and the use of props and set were introduced, the actors worked without masks. They would not put on the masks until they had become familiar with the scene and the objects.

Scenes which contained dialogue were first learnt by the actors (unmasked) and then by the mask characters. The script material, actions and words were then adjusted to suit the actor and character they were playing. Sometimes the script was purely a physical description of what happens For example, *'Columbina hops on Arlecchino's shoulders to become a ghost chasing Pantalone and scaring him'.*

Scene descriptions such as this might eventually be choreographed with set lines or may remain as an improvised scene in performance. These decisions were made in the last week of rehearsal.

With the introduction of design elements which I had built or acquired outside rehearsal times, the actors found new possibilities for comic business and status transactions between the characters. I also incorporated many props and set ideas brought into rehearsals by the actors, such as arm floaties, a wooden spoon and a rubber chicken.

We trained the mask characters to understand theatrical conventions like entrances and exits (in the Commedia no entrance or exit is ever ordinary), line cues and spatial awareness when more than one of them is on stage at once. It can be great fun trying to teach those egotistical mask characters some of the basic rules of stagecraft such as not standing in front of another character and listening for cues before speaking.

When working in Commedia, dialogue is delivered to the audience in a presentational style wherever possible. Once a character has established who they are talking to on stage, they can direct most of their dialogue towards the audience, occasionally looking back to the other character. This convention becomes natural after a while and ensures that the characters are constantly aware of and engaging the audience and that the masks are clearly seen. This differs from the conventions of Realism where the actor and characters do not acknowledge the presence of the audience and generally turn sideways or upstage from the audience while speaking.

Lecoq has some great exercises for actors to use during mask work so as to avoid unnecessary movement or shuffling by characters on stage. His training exercise, 'The Nine Attitudes', gives actors excellent choices for mask characters when they are momentarily stationary yet still involved in a scene. The attitudes allow a great economy of physical action but are highly evocative and suggestive for an audience. (Lecoq, 2001) We have translated these attitudes into the positions of Dynamic Stillness in Chapter 3 (p.61).

During the final two weeks of rehearsal and devising for *Stardust* we continued the warm-ups and ran circus and stage fight routines without masks being worn, before running them with masks. This ensured that the routines became second nature and minimised the risk of injury. We then layered in the actors' skills and contributions, such as songs, musical instruments, foreign language phrases and *lazzi*. We found places in the performance where actors needed to change character, masks and costumes and layered in *lazzi* and *burle* to cover these times. These also became opportunities for characters to interact directly with the audience.

During the last week we did several runs of *Stardust* still finding new material, places to interact with the audience and editing the script, because if you can say it physically in the Commedia instead of with words, then you ditch the words! During run-throughs I would call, 'Freeze. Look around you', to the actors on stage, to give them a moment to check their spatial arrangements with one another, mask protocols and sight lines for the audience, etc. Ideally, if you took a photograph every few seconds of the stage full of characters, the spatial relationships between them, their body postures and gestures would look like a beautifully composed painting or tableau, full of life and energy.

In the final days of rehearsal we invited industry colleagues and a target group from a local school to be an audience for a run-through of *Stardust.* After feedback from this audience, we accommodated many of their ideas during the final two days of rehearsal.

Conclusion

Whenever I am working on a new production I remember something the psychoanalyst, Carl Jung, once wrote: 'The creation of something new is not accomplished by the intellect but by the play instinct acting from inner necessity. The creative mind plays with the objects it loves.' This is especially true of the Commedia dell'arte and a project such as *Stardust.*

STARDUST SCENARIO

Stardust Island is a tropical, eco-tourism resort. It is owned and run by Dottore with the assistance of his adopted daughter Columbina, handyman Arlecchino and chef Pulcinella. A wealthy developer, Pantalone, hires the bullying Captain to intimidate Dottore, his staff and the guests (the audience). Pantalone wants them to abandon the island, acquire it for himself and build a cruise-ship terminal, high-rise apartments, marinas, airfields, golf courses, shopping malls and carparks to 'bring Stardust out of the dark ages'.

Arlecchino is sent by Dottore to the Gold Coast on the mainland to hire seven mean and tough people to help protect the island. Arlecchino engages Brighella who promises that his 'six brothers' will soon follow him to the island. The 'brothers' will back up Brighella and share in the 'seven unimaginable treasures' promised as payment by Dottore for ridding the island of Pantalone and the Captain.

This archetypal plot and theme can also be found in films such as the American 'western', *The Magnificent Seven*, the Japanese 'eastern', *The Seven Samurai*, and the animation, *A Bug's Life*. In *Stardust* the 'good guys' regain their honour through wit, slapstick, comic devices and audience engagement techniques while ensuring the island will be retained by Dottore in pristine condition. The play's setting also has some resonances with television's 'modern' equivalent of the Commedia dell'arte, 'Gilligan's Island'.

The Commedia characters in *Stardust* have been adapted from the Italian tradition and placed in a uniquely Australian context with particular reference to Queensland. I am, after all, a Queensland-based writer, director and actor, and influenced by the people I have encountered and the locations and situations in which I have found myself. The issue of conservation versus progress is not unique to Queensland, but certainly eco-tourism is topical when located somewhere tropical. And it goes without saying, that the themes of greed, love, vanity, bullying, hunger, heroism and revenge explored in *Stardust* are universal.

Steven Gration

Stardust was produced by Commotion Theatre Company and first performed in Brisbane in April 2000.
Original Cast:
  Mary Eggleston
    Il Dottore
    Columbina
    Pulcinella
    Woman on the Street
  Kurt Duvall
    Arlecchino
    The Captain
  Michael Sams or Nicky Peelgrane
    Pantalone
    Brighella
    Man on the Street
Written, Directed and Designed by Steven Gration

Helpful Hints

Stardust is structured to enable three actors to perform all the roles. Costume and mask changes are conducted behind a simple painted backdrop. The set, consisting of cube-shaped rostra for tables, chairs and a bar, allows for simplicity of use and location changes. The use of *lazzi* and *burle* assists in covering the time taken by the actors for costume and mask changes. Part of the delight for an audience is the realisation, at the end of the performance, that three actors have sustained the pace and energy of a play with nine characters.

Alternatively, the performance could be played by up to nine actors plus several musicians accompanying the action and/or providing music in the 'Stardust Island Bar and Grill' and 'Crazy's Bar' scenes. Additionally, musicians might wish to provide sounds to accompany actions such as hits, punches and falls. When a particular character enters, a music motif that belongs only to that character might accompany their entrance and/or exit.

Generally in Commedia, no object ever touches the ground when it is thrown or falls unless it is for comic or dramatic effect at the end of a *lazzo*, *burle* or slapstick sequence. If possible, any object falling to the ground should be accompanied by a musical or percussive noise.

The stage in Commedia performances should never be empty of players from the moment the performance begins until the play is finished and a curtain call taken. As the foot of one character leaves the stage, the audience should be seeing the foot and leg of another entering or the masked face of another character appearing. This convention reflects the playing style of the traditional Commedia troupes who performed in the marketplace or street and worked at a fast pace and high energy level to maintain the attention of their audiences so they were not tempted to wander away. If no one is on stage even for a brief moment, the audience may drift off because they think that nothing is going to happen or that the performance has ended.

STARDUST CANOVACCI

Scene List

1. A Stardust Welcome
2. Pantalone Pushes Progress
3. Pantalone Plays with the 'Guests'
4. Pantalone Places His Order
5. The Captain Makes His Presence 'Felt'
6. Dottore Cooks Up a 'Mean' Plan
7. Arlecchino Prepares for Travel and Pledges His Love
8. Arlecchino, Like a Duck to Water
9. Arlecchino Arrives on the Mainland
10. Arlecchino Meets Brighella
11. Arlecchino Carries Brighella Back to Stardust Island
12. Brighella Gets His Instructions
13. Brighella and the Captain Have Their First Skirmish
14. Columbina Puts Us All in the Picture
15. Columbina Overhears the Captain's Evil Plans
16. The Stardust Crew Plan Their Counter-Punch
17. The Battle Begins
18. The Cold Ghost Appears
19. The Kitchen Becomes a Battlefield
20. A Stardust Happy Ending

Sets for *Stardust* based on Director's Journal sketches.

STARDUST

The play opens on Stardust Island Resort. The exterior of the Bar and Grill.

1. A STARDUST WELCOME

Enter Dottore dressed in neck-to-knee bathers, bathing cap, pool-gown and snorkel. He is singing a pseudo-Latin song to the tune 'Strangers in the Night'.

DOTTORE:
Doobee doobee alpha,
Doo beta delta,
Doo bee doo bee theta—

[*Seeing the audience*] Oh! [*Calling*] The guests have arrived! Staff! Quickly! The guests! [*To the audience*] Um… Welcome everyone to Stardust Island Resort. Thank you for booking with us. We hope you have a lovely stay. [*Shouting*] Arlecchino?! Welcome music please! [*To the audience*] As you can see our island has been left in its natural state with cosy but humble cottages blending into the tropical surroundings. Tropicoitus non-interruptis!

Arlecchino enters dressed in a Hawaiian shirt, board shorts and carrying a ukelele.

Arlecchino. At last. The guests have arrived earlier than expected. Please welcome them with the arrival song. Ladies and gentlemen, our Entertainment Officer, Arlecchino. Oh and my humblest apologies, I am of course your host, Il Dottore Graziano. My adopted daughter, Columbina, will be with you shortly. She shall be your hostess during your stay. One day she shall inherit Stardust Island, the jewel in the crown of the Coral Sea. Arlecchino. Sing! [*Calling*] Columbina?! Columbina?!

He exits into the Stardust Bar and Grill.

ARLECCHINO: [*singing and strumming the ukelele*]
Welcome toooooo…
Stardust Island, to the Island,
We hope you have a lovely stay.
It's the Island, Stardust Island,
We've left it natural, that's our way.

You can snorkel on the reef,
Walk in the forest deep,

In the water brush your teeth,
Unwanted noise, not hear a peep.
You will have a lovely sleee-eeep.

It's the Island, Stardust Island,
No developer can touch.
It's nature's playground, meant for romance,
You'll fall in love here very much.

You can snorkel on the reef,
Walk in the forest deep,
In the water brush your teeth,
Unwanted noise, not hear a peep…

2. PANTALONE PUSHES PROGRESS

Pantalone enters wearing gold chains, a white suit and shoes. He puts his hand on the ukulele strings, silencing the song. This scares Arlecchino.

ARLECCHINO: Mr Pantalone!

PANTALONE: Yes. Yes. Yes. Prattle, prattle. La de da. This island is not so great. Where's the marina, the high-rise apartments with a view, the pool, spa, tennis courts, golf course, golf buggies, restaurants, casino, poker machines, shopping malls, carparks, jet skis, paragliding, cruise ship terminal…? Your stupid boss is living in the Dark Ages. Read my lips, Arlecchino. The 1990s are dead. It's a new decade. It hurts me to tell you, but the tooth—

Arlecchino interrupts.

ARLECCHINO: I know a good dentist.

PANTALONE: The two thousands!

ARLECCHINO: Two fountains? Oh, we have a natural spring and waterfall. We don't need two fountains, Mr Pantalone.

PANTALONE: The two thousands have arrived. The new millennium, you mullet-head.

Arlecchino sulks and goes to leave.

Aw. Did I hurt your feelings? I'll tell you what…

Columbina enters wearing denim shorts and a tank-top. She overhears Pantalone.

I'll pay you twice what the doctor pays you if you'll work for me.

ARLECCHINO: He pays me nothing.

PANTALONE: I'll pay you three times that!

ARLECCHINO: What would I do? Sing?

He strums the ukulele and sings.

This is Stardust Island, it's the—

PANTALONE: [*interrupting*] No! It's night-time work. Making noise, smashing things up. You're good at breaking things, aren't you?

He pats Arlecchino on the head and they nod in agreement.

COLUMBINA: He doesn't want to work with you, Mr Pantalone, he's happy with us.

Columbina puts her arm through Arlecchino's who shakes and nods his head at the same time. Pantalone gets horny at the sight of Columbina. His hands and tongue work overtime.

PANTALONE: Oh, Columbina. When you marry me we will inherit this island and make it a rich man's playground.

Pantalone tries to touch her and she whacks him, causing Pantalone and Arlecchino to fall to the ground.

COLUMBINA: Dream on, you old crayfish. I told you I'll never marry you. I love Arlecchino and when the Doctor hands the island over to me it will stay just as it is.

PANTALONE: We'll see... I have a friend visiting today who might just change your mind. Fetch the Doctor. Now!

3. PANTALONE PLAYS WITH THE 'GUESTS'

Arlecchino and Columbina exit while Pantalone improvises with the audience. He asks where they are from, makes fun of them and tries to incite them into agreeing that the island should be developed. He begins to harass the females in the audience. Finally, Dottore enters as Pantalone starts to brag about other resorts he has built.

Note: In performance the actor playing Pantalone may choose to talk about his recent developments in ecologically vulnerable areas including activities like logging, woodchipping, clearing of dunes and mangroves, building housing estates, siphoning water out of rivers, etc. as things he is proud of. The actor might choose topics that are relevant to the audience and/or the region the performance takes place in.

4. PANTALONE PLACES HIS ORDER

DOTTORE: Señor Pantalone. Welcome once again to our Stumble Hardust Island.

PANTALONE: 'Stumble Hardust Island'?

DOTTORE: I mean humble Stardust Island. Your wish is my command, for we turn away no one from our little piece of paradise, our jewel in the crown of the Coral Sea, our—

PANTALONE: Doctor! You're a very boring man. If my wish truly is your command, sell me this island, now! Today! I'll write out the cheque here and now.

DOTTORE: Well… that is… that is… impossible. I have bequeathed this island to Columbina. I am her guardian and she shall inherit this island in pristine condition.

PANTALONE: Great! Then she'll marry that idiot Arlecchino, they'll lose all their guests because of his incompetence, and I'll buy the island at a bargain basement price.

DOTTORE: If that is God's wish, so be it. But Arlecchino must prove he is worthy of Columbina before I shall allow them to marry.

PANTALONE: [*to the audience*] Ah! There's a great chance my plan will work. Arlecchino stuffs everything up. [*To Dottore*] Doctor, I have invited a very interesting guest here today. He's brave, wealthy and handsome. When he arrives, Columbina will change her mind about Arlecchino. And if she doesn't, I have other plans for all of you.

DOTTORE: Threatenus nofearem, Pantalone.

Note: Il Dottore often throws in these pseudo-Latin phrases. The actor playing Dottore should feel free to invent his/her own.

PANTALONE: We'll see. Get me some food. A banquet. My guest will be here soon. A pound of flesh for me and something to quench his thirst… [*Aside*] … preferably blood!

DOTTORE: As you desire, Shylock, I mean Pantalone. The banquet please, Pulcinella. Chop-chop. Our 'friend' Señor Pantalone and his 'soon to arrive' guest wish to wine and dine.

Dottore exits into the Bar and Grill.

5. THE CAPTAIN MAKES HIS PRESENCE 'FELT'

Pantalone sits at a small table with two chairs as the Captain enters. He is wearing an army disposal flak jacket and boots, with a super-soaker water gun slung over his shoulder. He salutes Pantalone and bounces into commando dives and rolls before making for the females in the audience. He tries to kiss their hands and threatens the males. The Captain addresses everyone in a strong American accent.

Note: The actor playing the Captain can insult the males in the audience in much the same way that a stand-up comedian insults a heckler. The actor should gather some of these put-downs and put them in their kit of insults!

CAPTAIN: I am Captain Cocodrillo ex-S.A.S., C.I.A., ASIO, ASIS, Viet-vet, Contra mercenary, Iraqi returnee. Twice. Now I work for… myself! I am the world's police but I only go where I am invited. Sometimes of course the invitation gets lost in the mail, but I go anyway. I create democracy and anyone who doesn't like it gets sent to prison in Cuba, without trial! We'll teach them how democracy works!

He approaches the audience.

Everybody loves me, everybody fears me, in peace [*He kisses a female's hand*] and in war.

He threatens a male with the super-soaker gun.

PANTALONE: Captain, join me. I have ordered a banquet.

CAPTAIN: [*saluting*] With pleasure, Pantalone. [*To a female*] I am sorry, my dear, I must interrupt this affair, for I have important business I must attend to…

He kisses her hand.

A man is not a camel!

He sits with a flourish and comments loudly on the audience.

Such pretty mermaids amongst a school of mullets. I may have to go 'fishing' later.

He winks and nudges Pantalone.

PANTALONE: The women down south are battered flakes compared to the fresh oysters up this way.

He provocatively wags his tongue.

CAPTAIN: I hope the banquet you have ordered is as delicious as the women!
PANTALONE: I doubt it.

Pulcinella, wearing a chef's coat and hat, enters with a tray of food.

Note: Try using the traditional rubber chicken (which is often used in slapstick comedy) as the food on the tray.

Captain, you go to work as of this moment.
CAPTAIN: Understood, Pantalone. Understood.

The Captain trips Pulcinella and the tray ends up on the ground.

Clumsy. Take it back. Get a fresh one.

Pantalone and the Captain snigger. Pulcinella exits, tail between his legs.

PANTALONE: Good work, Captain. This 'fearless' crew will beg me to take this island for free before you're finished with them.
CAPTAIN: For a price, I will fight for 'Truth, Justice and the Amway'.

Pulcinella re-enters with a fresh tray. The Captain trips him again.

Oops!

The Captain points back to the kitchen. Pulcinella seethes with anger as he heads back to the kitchen but stops halfway. In full view of the audience, but out of sight of the Captain or Pantalone, he spits and dribbles all over the food.

PANTALONE: I love your work, Captain Cocodrillo.
CAPTAIN: [*singing*]

I've only just begun to play,
Cheap lies, false promises
Show me the money
And then I'll stay.

Show me the money, Pantalone, you can do it. Come on!
PANTALONE: [*showing off his nose in profile to the audience*] It's Tom Cruise. The Prince of Kwa!

Pulcinella slams the tray onto the table before the Captain can trip him again. Pulcinella backs off and sniggers to the audience as the Captain tries the food.

CAPTAIN: Hmm! Not bad. What's this clear sauce? It's tasty, I'd like the recipe.

Pulcinella exits, sniggering without answering.

PANTALONE: [*he reluctantly hands a bag of money to the Captain.*] Tomorrow night, Captain, we go into Phase Two. You must exterminate the Doctor, seduce Columbina, and enslave Arlecchino and Pulcinella. We'll put them to work developing my island shovelling sh... concrete.

CAPTAIN:

Now is the winter of our discontent,
Made glorious summer by this son of a gun,
And all the clouds that rained upon our island
In the deep bosom of a woman buried…

Note: The actor playing the Captain can choose any number of Shakespeare's lines to misquote during the performance.

PANTALONE: Captain, leave the misquoting to the Doctor.

Columbina enters.

COLUMBINA: [*to the Captain*] I don't know who you are, but if you're going to be a guest on this island you will treat the staff with respect.

CAPTAIN: [*eating and looking at her*] Delicious! [*Putting out his hand*] I am Captain Cocodrillo. There must be a misunderstanding. Your chef… [*He grabs her hand*] … was so clumsy. I don't know what story he told you… [*He pulls her onto his lap*] … but I am an officer and a gentleman. You have no doubt heard of me. Down south I am a legend.

He looks at his crotch. Columbina struggles to get away, unsuccessfully. The Captain speaks to Pantalone.

One must play the line delicately when one is attempting to bring in the fish.

Columbina uses martial arts to break the Captain's hold and put him on the ground. She stands over him.

I like a fish that fights hard.

COLUMBINA: Consider me the one that got away! Mr Pantalone, please leave with your guest before I call security. The Doctor will hear about this.

She exits.

PANTALONE: [*laughing uncontrollably*] Get a doctor, I need a doctor, I'm sick… with laughter!

CAPTAIN: Pantalone, I hope she's not in charge of security on the island.

PANTALONE: No. It's a fool called Arlecchino. He's the Entertainment Officer, Tour Guide, Rubbish Collector, Lifeguard, Toilet Cleaner… He's incapable of doing anything without stuffing it up.

CAPTAIN: Hmmm. And tell me, why do they call their boss the Doctor?

PANTALONE: He has a Doctorate in Philosophy from some obscure university. I think all they do these days is train actors for television so most of their graduates are out of work.

Note: This could also be a comment on the HECS fees for university students and the Doctor having to pay it off for the rest of his life or any other comment on the changing nature of free education to 'user pays' education.

CAPTAIN: A university for real… unemployment.

PANTALONE: Philosophers and actors, who needs them! [*He looks at the audience.*] There's something in that for all of us.

Dottore enters.

DOTTORE: I must ask you and your guest to leave this island. You've upset my staff.

PANTALONE: So sorry. Doctor, this is the Captain. [*A fanfare*] De-de-de dum.

The Captain puts out his hand. Dottore nervously puts his out to shake hands. The Captain pulls his away and scares Dottore.

CAPTAIN: Boo!

PANTALONE: Come on, Captain, let's leave this mosquito-infested place. The trouble with this island, Dottore, is you've let nature take over, it's out there lurking.

Pantalone uses the rubber chicken to demonstrate man's control over nature doing World Wrestling moves on it, finally pinning it to the ground.

It's a one… two… three! Concrete. Concrete. How can you have progress without concrete?

DOTTORE: I disagree, Señor Pantalone.

PANTALONE: When I want your opinion, Doctor Dullard, I'll ask for it.

DOTTORE: Insultè no morè. Aleavè derci!

He points for them to leave.

CAPTAIN: I'll be back!

He pronounces it 'Bach' like Arnold Schwarzenegger.

DOTTORE: I don't care if you're Mozart or even Beethoven. Sayonara.

PANTALONE: You are a slug, Dottore.

DOTTORE: A slug, in fact, is a snail without the burden of a high-rise development on its back.

Pretending to be hurt by the last comment, Pantalone imitates 'The Elephant Man' and moves closer to Dottore.

PANTALONE: I am not an animal, I am a human being, love me.

CAPTAIN: [*pulling Pantalone back*] And a corpse, in fact, is a body without a head on it! See you soon, Doctor. It will take seven men to match me, whether it be fighting… [*He looks at a female in the audience and blows her a kiss*] … or f-f-fooing.

They exit laughing while Dottore paces up and down.

6. DOTTORE COOKS UP A 'MEAN' PLAN

DOTTORE: Something must be done. We are in grave danger. [*To the audience*] I am sorry for this nuisance, this intrusion. I hope this unpleasant scene will not be repeated. I shall take decisive action. I shall… I shall… What shall I do? Do you have any suggestions? How can I protect the island and Columbina and my staff…?

He solicits ideas from the audience, hopefully picking up on the idea of hiring someone to protect them. If the audience doesn't come up with the idea Dottore can suggest it for approval by the audience.

I'll send Arlecchino to the mainland, to the Gold Coast, to hire some protection. Some fighters who, for a price, will come to the island and defeat Pantalone and the Captain. I've been told the Gold Coast has the meanest people in the world. [*Calling*] Arlecchino!

Arlecchino enters.

Arlecchino, my life is in danger, Columbina's honour might be compromised, and you and Pulcinella may be enslaved to corporate developers unless we take immediate action.

ARLECCHINO: Huh?

DOTTORE: Pantalone has hired a bully to intimidate us into selling him Stardust Island.

Arlecchino is even more confused.

ARLECCHINO: Huh?!

DOTTORE: We're in deep sh… trouble.

ARLECCHINO: [*finally understanding*] Oh!

DOTTORE: Here's my plan…

He whispers in Arlecchino's ear but Arlecchino just laughs.

What's so funny?

ARLECCHINO: You tickled my ear.

Dottore gives up and talks at normal volume.

DOTTORE: You must leave tonight without anyone seeing you. Swim through the mangroves, row silently across the channel, then sail to the mainland, to the… Gold Coast, where you will find the meanest people on this planet. You must bring them back here to fight on our behalf to save Stardust Island. Have a rest and I shall arouse you after sunset.

ARLECCHINO: Oh, that's okay. Columbina usually arouses me after sunset.

DOTTORE: [*frowning and speaking to the audience*] I think there's not enough 'wooing' and too much 'fooing' on this island… [*Speaking to Arlecchino*] Very well, Columbina can see you safely away. She will give you the letter of contract. No doubt Pantalone and the Captain are keeping a watchful eye on me anyway.

Pantalone pokes his head quickly around the corner and disappears again.

Note: Whenever characters sense people spying on them, or hear a noise, they can launch into double takes. In this case, Dottore and Arlecchino can do a series of double takes looking around and at each other, just missing seeing Pantalone spying on them. These double takes can be choreographed or, better fun still, just improvised when circumstances arise throughout the performance.

Remember, find the seven meanest people on the Gold Coast. They won't be hard to find there. I will offer them a treasure beyond their imagination. You get fit for the journey, and if you succeed in this quest, you can marry Columbina.

7. ARLECCHINO PREPARES FOR TRAVEL AND PLEDGES HIS LOVE

Dottore exits into the Stardust Bar and Grill. Arlecchino does an Olympic Games athletic warm-up routine until Columbina enters. They do the 'love trapeze' movement, flitting across the stage as if each is on a flying trapeze, just missing each other as they pledge their love.

COLUMBINA: Oh, my love, you are going on a perilous, treacherous journey. Take care. Please return home with all your limbs and other bits. And be careful of sharks on the Gold Coast.

ARLECCHINO: Do not fear, Columbina, I will out-swim them.
COLUMBINA: I meant the sharks on the land.
ARLECCHINO: The Gold Coast does not scare me. I will bring back seven brave warriors to defend our island.

They stop their trapeze movements.

COLUMBINA: [*handing him a letter*] Here is the letter of contract. Under no circumstances open it. The contents are secret until you find the right people, the meanest people on the Gold Coast. Take care. If we succeed we will be together forever on Stardust Island.

They go to kiss but before they connect they launch into the 'I love you' lazzo.

I love you more than all the oceans.
ARLECCHINO: I love you more than all the fishes in the ocean.
COLUMBINA: I love you more than the Southern Sky.
ARLECCHINO: I love you more than all the stars in the sky.
COLUMBINE: I love you more than the cosmos.
ARLECCHINO: I love you more than the universe.
COLUMBINE: I love you more than infinity.
ARLECCHINO: I love your more than… [*He can't think of anything more.*] I just love you!

They go to kiss but a noise is heard. Columbina exits.

Note: The 'I love you' lazzo is as close as the lovers get to an argument by trying to outdo each other with the size of their love. The actors can devise their own 'I love you more than…' images or improvise it each time. Food is a good metaphor for the 'I love you' lazzo (e.g. 'I love you more than a Cherry Ripe', 'I love you more than a steamed dim sim').

8. ARLECCHINO, LIKE A DUCK TO WATER

Arlecchino launches into his 'travelling over the sea' lazzo while the set is transformed into Crazy's Cafe on the mainland at the Gold Coast.

Note: The actor playing Arlecchino mimes putting on arm-floaties, stretching, diving, swimming freestyle, backstroke, synchronised swimming, surfing, wiping-out, starting a motor on a rubber ducky, sailing, canoeing and finally collapsing on the shore. This lazzo is an improvisation with high energy encompassing all forms of water transport. It is fun if it is performed to some recorded classical music such as 'The William Tell Overture' or the 'Ride of the Valkyries'.

9. ARLECCHINO ARRIVES ON THE MAINLAND

When Arlecchino arrives on the Gold Coast it is dark and scary. Sounds of wind howling. A man walks past. Arlecchino steps in front of him.

ARLECCHINO: I'm very sorry to bother you, but would you have time to look at this letter of contract?

The man picks him up and throws him away. Arlecchino is crawling on the ground.

MAN: Go back to Sydney, cockroach. We've got enough scammers already on the Gold Coast.

ARLECCHINO: The Cold Ghost sure does have some mean people. I'm in luck!

A woman walks past in the opposite direction.

Madam, if you would be so kind as to look at this letter...

WOMAN: [*sweetly*] Oh, you poor thing, have you been retrenched? I'm afraid I'm just a tourist from Sydney...

She kicks him in the head, sending him flying.

So stop bothering me! Useless Queenslanders, you are cane toads and should be squashed. In Sydney we removed no-hopers like you, so tourists visiting the Olympics didn't have to vomit looking at you.

As Arlecchino recovers from his beating, the woman exits past Brighella who is hiding in a bin. He steals the woman's handbag without her noticing.

ARLECCHINO: The Dottore was right. I'm bound to find seven mean people on the Cold Ghost but how will I get them to read Dottore's letter of contract? I know, I'll open it myself, read the contents and tell them what the Doctor is offering.

Arlecchino launches into the 'reading the letter' lazzo.

Note: This is a classic lazzo where Arlecchino opens the sealed envelope and tries to read the letter. He professes the rest of the sequence aloud as he goes through the physical business of trying to re-seal the envelope.

Oh. I forgot I can't read. Now I will get into trouble for opening the envelope. I have to seal it again.

He licks it but the stickiness of the envelope is gone. He goes into a typical one-legged thinking pose. He has an idea.

I know. I am always hungry so I keep a supply of food on me. I have a bread crumb in my pocket. I'll chew on it and make it soggy and sticky and then I'll use it to stick the envelope closed.

He pulls a small piece of bread out of his pocket and starts to chew it, but on impulse swallows it.

Oh no! I was so hungry I ate it. Never mind, I have another piece hidden away.

He pulls it out of his sock and puts it into his mouth. The same thing happens. He swallows it.

Oh dear! That swim has made me very hungry. I ate it again. I have only one piece left.

He pulls it from the front of his trousers, having stored it down his undies. While the first two pieces are real bread, the third piece can, in fact, be made of a small piece of foam rubber to look like a piece of bread. He displays it to the audience.

I am not going to swallow this one. I've got an idea.

He goes to an audience member and pretends to pluck a hair from their head. He mimes tying the hair to the piece of (foam) bread. In fact, a piece of cotton is already attached to the foam and unwound by the actor as he mimes tying the hair. The 'bread' dangles from the 'hair' and Arlecchino puts the 'bread' in his mouth and wrapping the cotton around his tongue, he chews on the 'bread'… until he 'swallows' it. He then pulls the cotton out, unravelling it from his tongue to give the appearance he is drawing the bread back out of his tummy. He dangles it in front of the audience, smiling. He puts the envelope containing the letter on the floor and puts the bread on the back of it and stomps on the bread and the envelope with his foot. Before the show, the back of the envelope has been sprayed with the glue used to stick photographs to art-board. It is a clear glue and quite tacky. The envelope sticks to the sole of Arlecchino's shoe as he palms the bread and cotton back into his pocket. He then goes into comic antics trying to reach the envelope on the end on his shoe. He hops on one leg, stretches forward losing his balance going into a dive roll and backflip, if the actor can manage it!

Finally, he offers his foot to an audience member to take the envelope off the bottom of his shoe. He thanks them, puts the envelope on the floor and does the final sealing by sitting on it and bouncing up and down. Of course the envelope now sticks to his bottom, so when he stands up it is gone from the floor. He accuses audience members of stealing it until they point out it is not only behind him, it is stuck to his behind. He reaches between his legs, his bottom facing the audience, and grabs it. He thanks the audience for their help.

As he finishes, Brighella's voice is heard mumbling from the bin as he empties the woman's bag and appears again.

10. ARLECCHINO MEETS BRIGHELLA

ARLECCHINO: Phew. Now to find a mean person.
BRIGHELLA: Dirty deeds da da dum dum dum…
ARLECCHINO: This could be one of the people we're looking for… I wonder if he'll do it dirt cheap? [*Calling from a distance so he doesn't get hurt*] Excuse me, sir.

Brighella looks around thinking Arlecchino must be talking to someone else.

Yes, sir. You!
BRIGHELLA: Yeah, what? I done nothin'.
ARLECCHINO: Would you please read this letter? It could change your life.
BRIGHELLA: You Mormons are getting desperate. Doesn't anyone answer their door anymore?
ARLECCHINO: There could be untold treasures for you, if you are chosen.
BRIGHELLA: Oh, you're from the casino. Why didn't you say so? I'll have a go at your lucky dip.

Brighella snatches the letter and opens it, eating the bread crumb Arlecchino has sealed the envelope with, and then reads the letter.

Seven meanest… fight bad guys… Capitano and Pantalone… offer treasure beyond imagination… Stardust Island Resort… signed Dottore, care of bearer Arlecchino. When do we leave?
ARLECCHINO: You'll do it?
BRIGHELLA: Whatever.
ARLECCHINO: But I need six others who'll share the treasure.
BRIGHELLA: Share! I don't wanna share… I want it all!
ARLECCHINO: I'm under strict orders to hire seven. You must know six others.
BRIGHELLA: [*he has an idea*] Yeah. I do. My bruvvers. Six of them. Wait a second. I'll fetch 'em.

He launches into the lazzo of 'being his six brothers'. This involves calling to his 'brothers' in a bin and answering in a different voice.

Hey Fred. Do ya wanna come?

[*Answering*] Yeah, I'll come.
Joe?
[*Answering*] Yeah, sure.
Billy, Jimmy, ah… what's yer name and thingo…?
[*Answering*] Yep. Yeah. No worries. I'm in!
[*To Arlecchino*] See, me an' me six bruvvers will do it.

ARLECCHINO: Gee, that was lucky all your brothers were here.

BRIGHELLA: Don't you have… [*He spins the bin around to show the sign.*] … Brotherhood bins where you come from? We're the brothers from the hood.

ARLECCHINO: We'd better head back before daylight, while the Captain and Pantalone are still asleep. I'll take you across one at a time.

BRIGHELLA: Remind me where we're going again.

ARLECCHINO: Stardust Island,

He bursts into song.

It's the Island,
We hope you have a lovely stay…

BRIGHELLA: [*interrupting*] Yeah. Whatever. Anything's gotta be better than Surface Parasite on a Saturday night. I'll go with you now. My 'six brothers' will get their own way across later…
[*He calls down the bin.*] Won't you, boys?
[*He echoes their voices.*] Yeah. Sure. See you there. No worries. Gotcha. Catch ya 'ron.

Arlecchino sets up to take Brighella back to Stardust Island doing the reverse of the 'travelling over the sea' lazzo. Brighella speaks to the audience.

Seven treasures beyond my imagination, all for me…

He holds up the woman's handbag and addresses the audience.

I am not a thief. I am an ingenious calculator who finds an object before its owner has lost it.

11. ARLECCHINO CARRIES BRIGHELLA BACK TO STARDUST ISLAND

Brighella leaps onto Arlecchino's back for the journey to Stardust Island. The set is transformed during their travels.

Note: The 'travelling over the sea' lazzo on the return voyage can involve slapstick and clowning routines including send-ups of films such as the 'I'm the king of the world' sequence from 'Titanic'.

12. BRIGHELLA GETS HIS INSTRUCTIONS

As they arrive, bedraggled from the sea crossing, Dottore enters and completes the set change back from Crazy's Cafe on the Gold Coast to the Stardust Island Resort. The change is done as though Dottore is opening up in the morning, like in the first scene of the play.

DOTTORE: Doobee doobee alpha beta delta…

Dottore sees Brighella holding Arlecchino upside down in a tangle. Dottore thinks it is a monster like the scene in Shakespeare's 'The Tempest', when Stephano sees Caliban and Trinculo in a tangle.

Catherine! Zeta! Jones! What monster has been sent to torment me?
ARLECCHINO: Dottore.

He struggles from beneath Brighella.

It's me, Arlecchino. I have brought back a mean man.
DOTTORE: Here's my comfort. But, Arlecchino, I asked you to find seven.
ARLECCHINO: His six brothers will follow soon.
DOTTORE: Maximus Gloriosus! Welcome, um… ah… Your name, sir?

Brighella looks around.

BRIGHELLA: Who? Aw, me? Brighella, at your service.
DOTTORE: Excellent. Now these are the rules. The Captain, who has been hired by Pantalone to bully us off the island because we won't sell it to him, will try to provoke you into a fight. You must not touch him first or Pantalone will have his lawyers charge you with assault. However, if the Captain ever touches you or one of your brothers, you can retaliate under the protection of the law of self defence. Clear?
BRIGHELLA: Don't touch first.
DOTTORE: Good. Now disguise yourself as a singer and when your brothers arrive they can pretend they're in your band. We'll use the element of surprise. I'll get Pulcinella to take your food order. You must be hungry.
BRIGHELLA: [*to Dottore*] I like it here already. When do I… I mean, me and my six bruvvers, get the seven unimaginable treasures?
DOTTORE: When the Captain is defeated and Pantalone agrees to leave us alone. Arlecchino, get Brighella the ukelele and find Columbina. [*He exits. Calling*] Pulcinella! Columbina!
ARLECCHINO: [*hugging the ukelele*] Columbina, Columbina.
BRIGHELLA: [*to Arlecchino*] Who's this Columbina?

ARLECCHINO: She's more beautiful than an Eskimo Pie. And when we succeed in the plan to get rid of the Captain, the Doctor will let me marry her and give us the island to run together.
BRIGHELLA: I hate happy endings.

He makes a vomit sign as Arlecchino gives him the ukelele and exits. Brighella wipes it, then strums a few chords until Pulcinella enters with a tray of food.

G'day, mate.

Pulcinella is scared.

Don't be frightened, little fella. I'm on your side. I'm a good guy… for once… I think. What's your name?
PULCINELLA: Pulcinella.

They shake hands as the Captain enters.

13. BRIGHELLA AND THE CAPTAIN HAVE THEIR FIRST SKIRMISH

CAPTAIN: Oh, how sweet. Isn't love a wonderful thing? Pulcinella, get me some takeaway chicken, now.

Pulcinella shakes and runs off.

Who the hell are you? You are the ugliest creature I have ever seen. You look like you've been dragged out of a Brotherhood bin.

Brighella starts to fume.

Got no tongue to match no brain. I asked who you are… Are you always so rude, sir? [*To the audience*] Sir! What a joke! Sir!
BRIGHELLA: [*seething*] I'm Brighella, the new musician.
CAPTAIN: I can guess the only instrument you're capable of playing and it's not musical. Ha ha! Get it!

Brighella has had enough and is about to clobber him when Dottore comes rushing between them.

DOTTORE: What's going on? Brighella, remember what I said.

Brighella is right in the Captain's face.

BRIGHELLA: Not touching! Not touching!
CAPTAIN: I think you're up to something, Dottore. If he's a musician, let's hear a

song and hurry Pulcinella up with my takeaway chicken. Put it on Pantalone's account, I'm not wasting my hard-earned money on living expenses.

The Captain plays with the bag of money on his belt. Dottore nods to Brighella to play a song. He launches into lyrics based on a Sinatra combination.

BRIGHELLA:

Start spreading the glue,
Make a coffin today,
I'm gonna slice the Captain up, like pork, like pork.
I wanna wake up to the sound of screaming
In a city full of creeps,
And find a pile of dead bodies,
Bullies and critics, sliced into strips.
It's my way, or the highway.

CAPTAIN: Very smart. Be careful, my man. If you're still here at midnight you may find yourself floating upside down in the swamp like the Doctor.

Pulcinella arrives with a rubber chicken.

I ordered takeaway chicken. Where's the lunch wrap?

Pulcinella shrugs. The Captain tickles Pulcinella's feet and arms with the chicken to make him dance.

See, ladies and gentlemen. Rap. The lunch rap! Just tickling, just tickling. Thanks for the dancing.

Pulcinella is furious with the Captain. Brighella steps in between them.

Thanks for the music. Be ready to face some of your own tonight.

As the Captain walks off with the chook Pulcinella wants to kill him. Brighella stops Pulcinella.

BRIGHELLA: Easy, little fella. His time will come. Besides, look at this…

Brighella shows him the money bag he stole from the Captain while he was teasing Pulcinella. Pulcinella exits laughing. Brighella hums a few more bars of his song. Brighella speaks to the audience and asks questions about the island, the Captain, Pantalone, etc. until Columbina and Arlecchino enter, in love.

14. COLUMBINA PUTS US ALL IN THE PICTURE

COLUMBINA: Arlecchino, you are so brave. If we can scare Pantalone and the Captain off with the seven mean— [*She sees Brighella.*] I mean brave warriors you brought back, we can marry and live on the island forever.

Brighella hides the money on his belt.

ARLECCHINO: This is Brighella. He's come from the Cold Ghost to help us.
COLUMBINA: Welcome, sir.

Brighella looks around.

BRIGHELLA: Oh, yeah. Whatever.
COLUMBINA: Where are your six brave companions?
BRIGHELLA: Who? Oh, um. My six bruvvers? They're getting their own way over. They'll be here later.
COLUMBINA: You two rest up. I think we're in for a tough night. Plan your strategy inside and I'll keep a lookout.
BRIGHELLA: She's nice.
ARLECCHINO: Yes. We love each other more than… more than…
BRIGHELLA: Yeah, whatever. I always need at least two women to satisfy me. Hey, tell me about the treasures beyond my imagination I am going to get.
ARLECCHINO: [*as they exit…*] The Doctor hasn't told me exactly what it is, but I am sure it will be very good.
COLUMBINA: [*to the audience*] Even if we defeat Pantalone and the Captain, we still have one major problem. We don't have enough money to keep the island running. I've just been doing the accounts and the Doctor doesn't realise we haven't the cash flow to keep going without turning the island totally commercial. And the GST is a nightmare. So much for 'There will never, ever be a GST'! It's destroying the tourist industry. Those nasty Democrats sold us out without even consulting us, and add the Queensland Government's policy of no daylight saving in summer, it's killing us.

That was the didactic bit of the play. The intention is to open up discussion amongst the audience on important issues. The playwright does not necessarily subscribe to the political views just spoken. Written and authorised by Columbina for the playwright.

I don't know how the Doctor intends to pay Brighella or his six brothers… Oh well. I guess we'll have to solve one problem at a time.

She launches into a popular song of hope for a better tomorrow. Captain and Pantalone are heard entering. Columbina hides.

15. COLUMBINA OVERHEARS THE CAPTAIN'S EVIL PLANS

CAPTAIN:

Tomorrow and tomorrow and tomorrow
Creeps in this petty pace from day to day
To the last snail of recorded time.

PANTALONE: Yes. Yes. [*To the audience*] Misquote. [*To the Captain*] Captain, what is the plan to finish this lot off swiftly and without fuss?

CAPTAIN: After sunset we return. You keep watch outside. I'll sneak inside and eliminate the Doctor. When the others see his lifeless body they'll come out screaming with me in pursuit. You make the offer to take over the island, enslave Arlecchino and Pulcinella, and give Columbina to me while they're all still in shock at the Doctor's untimely death. Have the other half of the money with you. I want it the moment the job's done.

PANTALONE: Simple.

CAPTAIN: I am the greatest.

They laugh as they exit.

Hey. Have you seen the first bag of money you gave me? I seem to have misplaced it.

COLUMBINA: [*correctly quoting Shakespeare*]

… But man proud man,
Dressed in a little bit of authority,
Most ignorant of what he's most assured,
His glassy essence, like an angry ape
Plays such fantastic tricks before high heaven
As makes the angels weep; who, with our spleens
Would all themselves laugh mortal.

Brighella and Arlecchino enter.

16. THE STARDUST CREW PLAN THEIR COUNTER-PUNCH

COLUMBINA: Listen! I've just heard the Captain and Pantalone plotting. This is what they're going to do…

They go into a huddle, she whispers, Arlecchino giggles, they look at him, he scratches his ear.

ARLECCHINO: It tickles…

Back into the huddle, Columbina finishes.

BRIGHELLA: This is what we have to do. Columbina, get the Doctor to go for a walk. Find an excuse for him to stay out all night.

COLUMBINA: I know. The baby turtles are about to hatch on the other side of the island. I'll ask the Doctor to watch over them to make sure no one harms them. He'll stay out all night. He loves the turtles and the dolphins and the birds and the fish and—

BRIGHELLA: Whatever. Sounds good. I'll take the Doctor's place inside and scare the shh… daylights out of the Captain. You take care of Pantalone outside. Do it like this…

Brighella whispers, Arlecchino giggles, they look at him.

ARLECCHINO: Shouldn't we wait for your six brothers?

BRIGHELLA: Who? Oh, um. No. This plan works best with just us. We'll… call them for back-up if we need them. Positions!

Arlecchino and Columbina scatter. Brighella sings and talks to himself.

'Slice the Captain up, like pork, like pork…' Treasures beyond your imagination, Brighella.

He plays with the money bag and talks to the audience.

This is a very good start. Just wait till I get hold of the Captain. And when he's gone I'll get the seven unimaginable treasures. I can't imagine what they are…

He exits inside the Stardust Bar and Grill. Dottore enters, calling back to Brighella.

DOTTORE: Good evening, Brighella. [*To the audience*] I'm off to take care of the taby burtles, I mean baby turtles. They're hatching on the other side of the island. They are cutus beautus. Mother Nature, you are a wondrous woman… phenomenologically speaking.

Sayanora, auf Wiedersehen, ciao…

He exits.

17. THE BATTLE BEGINS

The Captain bounces in commando-style, like in his opening entrance.

CAPTAIN: Pantalone, the coast is clear, so is the diner. Take up your surveillance position.

He points behind the bar.

PANTALONE: Yes. Yes. Let's get this over with and make the island mine.
CAPTAIN: Stay there. Make the secret sound if someone comes.

Pantalone practises chicken noises.

Good. Our work begins.
Life's but a walking shadow,
A poor player that struts and frets his hour upon the stage
And then is heard no more.
It is a tail held by an idiot,
Full of sound and fury signifying everything.

PANTALONE: Misquote!
CAPTAIN: Is not.
PANTALONE: Is!
CAPTAIN: Is not!
PANTALONE: Is!

They pause in a stand off, then…

CAPTAIN: Have you got the other half of my money?
PANTALONE: It's here. [*He shows a money bag on his belt.*] Finish the job first.
CAPTAIN: Okay, positions! Doctor, death is at your door!
PANTALONE: Doctor Death is at my door?
CAPTAIN: [*shaking his head*] Doctor, death doth come to your door.
PANTALONE: Doctor Death dot com to my door?
CAPTAIN: Forget it. Keep your eyes on the windows.
PANTALONE: Doctor Death dot com is on Windows?

The Captain gives up and enters the Bar and Grill. Pantalone tries to get comfortable hiding below the window but can't.

PANTALONE: Ow! I can't stay here, it's too uncomfortable. I'm going to sit over here.

He sits on a chair downstage.

Nothing will get past me. Every sense is as sharp as a toothpick, nerves of concrete, night vision like a… a…

18. THE COLD GHOST APPEARS

Pantalone falls asleep and snores. Columbina and Arlecchino enter side by side, hiding under Dottore's bathrobe. They play a game of 'sneaky ups', similar to the children's game 'Grandma's Footsteps', while Pantalone continues to sleep and snore. Columbina points to the money bag, but each time Arlecchino reaches out to grab it, Pantalone stirs and, half asleep, mumbles.

PANTALONE: Two fountains…
The year is two fountains…
Sea turtles…
Turtle soup…
Duck soup… Marx Brothers… very funny…

Pantalone sees the outline of Columbina and Arlecchino's heads. They huddle close together and freeze each time he mumbles and stirs.

Fruit bat… two heads…
Ugly little fella…

Arlecchino squeaks in fear of being discovered.

Speech impediment too…

Pantalone suddenly sits bolt upright.

Night vision like a hawk!

Columbina jumps up on Arlecchino's shoulders and throws the bathrobe over them both to form a tall, ghost-like figure. Pantalone sees it and freezes.

ARLECCHINO: I am a cold ghost.
PANTALONE: The dead Doctor's ghost!
[*Quoting Shakespeare*] The time has been
That when the brains were out
The man would die and there an end:
But now they rise again.
COLUMBINA: Misquote!
PANTALONE: Is not! But…
Thou canst not say I did it!
Never shake thy gory locks at me.
GHOST: Show me the money!
PANTALONE: Here take it. Spare me please!

He drops the money at their feet.

GHOST: Boo!

Pantalone runs away. Columbina and Arlecchino jump down and pick up the money bag. A loud noise is heard from inside.

COLUMBINA: Arlecchino, go inside and help Brighella. I'll make sure Pantalone doesn't return.

19. THE KITCHEN BECOMES A BATTLEFIELD

Arlecchino runs inside but immediately comes flying out the door or window in a dive roll. Columbina rushes to his aid. Brighella sticks his head out.

BRIGHELLA: Sorry, little buddy, my mistake.

Arlecchino rushes back in with Brighella. Lots of screams, yells, crashes, etc. while Columbina responds vocally and in gesture outside each time there is a sound of a punch or scream. Finally the Captain comes flying out, holding a sawn-off bread stick. Brighella follows holding a large knife. Columbina runs inside to check Arlecchino.

COLUMBINA: Arlecchino, are you all right? I love you more than an apple pie.
BRIGHELLA: [*lifting the Captain by the front of his jacket*] Now I'm touching. Touching.
CAPTAIN: Please let me go. I think I have a train to catch, a bus to catch, a plane to catch?

Brighella drops the Captain.

BRIGHELLA: Promise never to bother these people or visit this island again.
CAPTAIN: Promise. Cross my heart and hope to d… disappear for ever.
BRIGHELLA: Sir.
CAPTAIN: Sir.
BRIGHELLA: Let it be known… [*Quoting Shakespeare*] I was not of woman born!

Brighella pulls a monster pose. The Captain starts to crawl away but Pulcinella comes running in, letting out a martial arts scream, bashes the Captain with a rubber chicken and shoves a wooden spoon between his buttocks. The Captain exits, crawling in great pain.

Good onya, little buddy. Don't get mad, get even. Do you feel better?

Pulcinella nods and exits with a spring in his step. Brighella looks at his bag of money and laughs.

And now for my seven treasures beyond the imagination. I can't imagine what they'll be.

He sings.

Blood is in the air,
Spraying all around,
Blood is everywhere,
On my hands and on the ground…

Arlecchino enters.

ARLECCHINO: Well done, Brighella. We didn't even need your six brothers. Has the Captain gone?

Brighella nods.

BRIGHELLA: Yeah. I haven't had so much fun since I got thrown out of the blue light disco during schoolies week.

ARLECCHINO: Schoolies? That must have been a long time ago?

BRIGHELLA: Yeah, it was last year and 2006 and '98, '97, '96, '95… '89… it's all a bit of a haze really. It seems like ages.

Dottore enters.

20. A STARDUST HAPPY ENDING

DOTTORE: Doobee doobee doo…

ARLECCHINO: Doctor, you'll never guess what happened while you were watching the turtles…

DOTTORE: Um. Pantalone and the Captain attacked you and Brighella and his brave brothers defeated them.

ARLECCHINO: No.

DOTTORE: I knew that was too good to be true.

ARLECCHINO: We defeated them without Brighella's brothers. Me, Columbina, Pulcinella and Brighella did it on our own.

DOTTORE: Oh happy, happy, joy, joy. As promised, Arlecchino, you may marry Columbina and run the island together. Brighella, the seven unimaginable treasures are all yours.

BRIGHELLA: Yes!… What are the treasures?

DOTTORE: You may watch the sunrise from the beach on our island, seven days a week. I'll go and tell Columbina the good news.

BRIGHELLA: I don't get it. Ripped off! What's so unimaginable and treasury about a sunrise seven days a week?!

ARLECCHINO: I'm not real smart, Brighella, but I think what the Doctor means is, you don't have to go back to the Cold Ghost. You can stay on Stardust Island for as long as you wish.

BRIGHELLA: Here?!...Yahoo!

He runs around like an excited child.

Groovy baby, yeah!

Columbina enters.

COLUMBINA: Brighella, I've just heard the wonderful news. Are you going to stay with us?

BRIGHELLA: [*being cool*] Maybe.

COLUMBINA: Arlecchino, the Doctor said we could marry and run the island together.

ARLECCHINO: I love you.

COLUMBINA: There's one major problem. We've only got half the money we need to keep the island open.

She holds up Pantalone's money bag.

Even though Pantalone gave us this, we'll have to sell the island anyway.

She and Arlecchino take up a 'miserable' pose. Brighella thinks hard and then reluctantly...

BRIGHELLA: All right. Give a fella a guilt trip! I stumbled across this recently. I think the Captain would like you to have it.

He hands over the second bag and Columbina hugs him.

COLUMBINA: Oh, Brighella, you're lovely. Will you be our friend on this island forever?

BRIGHELLA: [*to the audience*] I normally hate happy endings because I'm never involved in any. [*Pause as he thinks.*] Yeah, I'll stay. Come here, you two, I feel a song coming on.

He lifts Columbina and Arlecchino onto his hips and they sing.

ALL:

It's the Island, Stardust Island,
We hope you had a lovely stay.
Stardust Island, it's the island,
We left it natural, that's our way...

THE END

Writer-Director's Afterword

A few years after creating the Commedia play *Stardust*, I became involved in community actions to save coastal parkland and beaches from commercial development and the construction of a ship terminal on the Southport Spit, Gold Coast, Queensland. A dedicated website, www.saveourspit.com, documents the fight to save public open space, surfing beaches, dive-sites, marine animals and coastal waters from massive development and restrictions to public access on The Spit. The real and ongoing story of saving The Spit has paralleled many of the issues explored in *Stardust*. Rather than art imitating life, this was a case of life imitating art! The Commedia dell'arte is at its strongest when it pre-empts or reflects important contemporary issues. For more information, see www.saveourspit.com.

CHAPTER 8

Bog In: Help for Educators

COMMEDIA IN THE DRAMA COURSE

Commedia activities are suitable for all levels of schooling (see Chapters 3 and 5 for suitability ratings for activities), not only within a unit on Commedia, but also within units on Clowning, Physical Theatre, Comedy, Shakespeare, Storytelling, Absurd Theatre, Improvisation, to name a few. All students respond to the inherent silly-ness of Commedia and the larger-than-life exuberance of its characters.

Generally, the older the students, the better the quality of Commedia performance, although naturally there are always exceptions! Senior High School students seem very suited for full-scale Commedia productions. At this age, they are better versed in the nuance, satire and wit required of the characters and the concept of countermask can be more successfully explored. They are also better equipped to handle the responsibility of organising the complexity of tasks required for a 'show'.

Senior High School students study critical literacy in English and similar concepts in other subject areas. At the same time, most of these students develop an ability to perceive the world as neither black nor white, but liberally infused with shades of grey (depending on where you're standing, of course). These steps toward maturity beautifully complement studies in Commedia. We believe Senior High School is the most appropriate time to fully explore Commedia. But that doesn't mean it can't be dipped into earlier in the educational process.

Commedia Schmedia—Why Study it? Rationale:

> One really nice thing about Commedia is that no one is debarred; you can never be too young or too old, too fat or too thin, too tall or

> too short, too ugly or too beautiful. Oddness of form or feature, even disabilities, can be turned to advantage, and if you show the ability to play Commedia, the troupe welcomes you.
>
> (Grantham, 2000)

Commedia is an excellent means for exploring the roots of comedy. Through it we can examine our impulse for laughter, an aspect of our humanity that deserves investigation and experimentation in order to try and make some sense of our crazy world. Within this course of study, Commedia helps students with later learning in other theatre traditions.

Experiences and Skills Gained by Studying Commedia

Through study in Commedia, students are able to:

- Explore and manage the elements of drama to make and shape dramatic action;
- Select and use appropriate acting techniques for the selected style of Commedia dell'arte;
- Manage and manipulate a mask appropriately;
- Develop ensemble skills; and
- Make analytical links to other dramatic forms and traditions such as Epic Theatre, Physical Theatre, Political Theatre, Community Theatre, Absurd Theatre, Shakespearean and Elizabethan Theatre, Asian Theatre, Clowning, Symbol and Ritual, Naturalism and Realism.

SOME IDEAS FOR ASSESSMENT

The following suggestions are basic ideas for educators to consider and elaborate upon when devising assessment or culminating tasks. This list is by no means prescriptive or exhaustive. Obviously, it is up to individual teachers to follow appropriate State or Territory syllabus guidelines and criteria when devising tasks.

At the time of writing, attempts to unify syllabuses under a national umbrella (*The Arts: A Curriculum Profile for Australian Schools* and *The Arts: A Statement on the Arts for Australian Schools* written by Curriculum Corp. in 1994) have been incomplete due to changes in government bureaucracy, although the concept of Key Learning Areas has been uniformly adopted. As a result, descriptors for Drama in each State are fundamentally the same, only the wording is different. In Queensland, for example, P-10 (Junior) and Senior Drama are divided into Forming, Presenting and Responding. In New South Wales, it's Making, Performing and Critically Studying; in South Australia, it's Arts Practice, Analysis and Response and Arts in Context. And so on.

Whatever your State or Territory, there exists a mode for making and shaping drama, a mode for performance and a mode for reflection and analysis of dramatic forms.

In order to accommodate all States, this Chapter divides ideas for assessment tasks into these three headings:

- Making and Shaping Drama
- Performance
- Reflection and Analysis of Dramatic Forms

The assessment or culminating task ideas presented below are given suitability ratings using the codes utilised in Chapters 3 and 5:

{LP} = Lower Primary: Early Childhood–Year 2
{P} = Primary: Years 3–6
{M} = Middle School: Years 6–10
{S} = Senior High School/Tertiary

Obviously, some class groups will be more advanced and want to try more challenging activities, while others will need more guidance.

Making and Shaping Drama—Assessment Possibilities

The following assessment activities are graded for their suitability at various levels of education using the above-mentioned codes.

The Fantastical Circus Birthday Party {LP}:

At this age, student work should not be for public viewing. After the teacher has demonstrated a few Commedia characters in role, or after the students have watched a Commedia performance, students create their own fantastical clown characters. These can be based on the criteria of voice, movement, obsessions/interests, mask (they could make their own), special tricks and costume. They are preparing their clown characters to attend the Fantastical Circus Birthday Party. The characters are all members of Fantastical Circus which has been running for ten years and everyone is celebrating. Students interact at the party in role. The teacher is in role as the dour Circus Accountant who announces that the Circus is going to close down because of a lack of finances. What happens next?

Make and Shape a Commedia Scene {P}:

Students devise a short Commedia scene between two characters based on a choice of theme: love, money or food. Students may combine these themes if they wish. They demonstrate status and then a status reversal. The scenes could be shared in a mini Commedia Oz Festival in the classroom.

Commedia Oz and Technology {P, M}:

This activity has students directing as well as making and shaping scenes in groups. Each group writes a *canovacci* (list of scenes) for a Commedia play. Once they have been approved by the teacher, the directors organise the actors in devising a series of freeze frames (up to four or five) of key moments of action in their plays. Once the freeze frames have been organised, the directors take digital photos of them so that they can be uploaded to a fictitious Commedia Oz website. The photographs, as well as the written *canovacci*, form their assessment. Students will obviously need to be instructed to make sure the actors are properly in role and that their freezes indicate action, character and suggest a storyline. This assessment is based on the storyboarding technique used in the film and television industries.

Oops! {M}:

A Commedia character/s gets 'caught' on stage while looking for the toilets. What happens next? Students devise a monologue/duologue to show an audience, using appropriate characterisation, voice, movement, physical attributes, personality traits, and relationships with other characters and audience interaction. The funniest monologues/duologues will be selected to appear in *Stardust II—Disaster in Paradise.*

Playwriting {M, S}:

Individually, students are to write a list of scenes (*canovacci*) for a Commedia performance based on a choice of given themes (e.g. unrequited love) or titles (e.g. 'The Great BBQ Fiasco'). From these listed scenes, they are to choose one scene to write in detail. It must contain two to three Commedia characters and at least one example of a *lazzo* (with detailed stage directions) and several examples of *burle*. Students should demonstrate appropriate characterisation, dialogue, movement, physical attributes, personality traits, and relationships with other characters. The detailed scene and *canovacci* are for entry into a playwriting competition where winners will have their work produced by the 'Commedia Oz Theatre Troupe'.

Constraints {M, S}:

Students are auditioning for a role in the modern Commedia troupe, 'Commedia Oz'. Give students constraints (e.g. night scene, disguise), then let them devise a performance in a modern context (see Chapter 5). Students should use appropriate characterisation, voice, movement, physical attributes, personality traits, and relationships with other characters.

{M} **adaptation:** Give students fewer ingredients (perhaps only four instead of the nine listed in Chapter 5) and less characters to manage with more lesson time to devise.

Choose your own adventure {S}:

This option acknowledges the skills that technology-savvy students have in allowing them to design their own assessment task. Students are asked to devise their own Commedia performance using their knowledge of the internet and cyberspace. Students are given the opportunity to create their own style and form in Commedia. For example, a student could devise a scenario where one or more Commedia characters gets sucked into cyberspace and lost. It is up to the other characters who remain on stage to find the cyberspace character/s. The 'lost' character/s could be projected onto a screen behind the live characters and interact with the live characters on stage. Possibilities for exploration using technology are endless and students are only limited by their own imagination.

Directing {S}:

Students are in role as a director from the acclaimed 'Commedia Oz Theatre Troupe' and all direct a scene from *Stardust* with updated jokes or all direct a brief scene (*canovaccio*) of their own invention. Within the directing activity, they must communicate their overall vision for the play, knowledge of appropriate character attributes, voice, movement and relationships with other characters.

Audition {S}:

Students audition for a position in the highly-acclaimed theatre troupe 'Commedia Oz', a company which specialises in traditional characters in modern contexts. In role as one of the modern masked characters, they perform their own prepared monologue to the Artistic Director of Commedia Oz. Within the monologue, students must communicate knowledge and understanding of character including physical attributes, personality traits, language, relationships with other characters, countermask, and motivations.

Performance—Assessment Possibilities

The following assessment activities are graded for their suitability at various levels of education.

The Fantastical Circus Birthday Party {LP}:

(Refer to this exercise in the Making and Shaping Drama section above)

During the drama that the students create, there should be an opportunity to observe students 'sharing' their work with one another. For instance, they might share their special tricks, or play at devising a special trick together. After the news of the closure of the Circus is announced, the students may decide to create an extra special show that will lure a huge audience.

Short Scenarios {P}:

Students are given short scenarios—or they may like to devise their own—to rehearse and polish for inclusion in a Commedia Oz Festival. Examples of these short scenarios are to be found in Chapter 5 (see pp.92–93).

Constraints {M, S}:

Students are auditioning for a role in the modern Commedia troupe, Commedia Oz. Students form small groups (2–3 actors). Give students constraints (e.g. night scene, disguise), then let them devise a performance in a modern context (see Chapter 5). Students should use appropriate characterisation, voice, movement, physical attributes, personality traits, and relationships with other characters. The first performance can be treated as a dress rehearsal after which the teacher can give feedback to help shape and polish students' work. The second performance is their assessment.

Please note: It is important to give students a few weeks to work together in assessment groups before the performance date so that they have sufficient opportunity to develop improvisation elements and finesse their scripted sections. The concept of using both improvisation and script comes first from the idea of the *Zibaldone* (a book passed down from generation to generation filled with monologues, poems, etc.) in traditional Commedia.

{M} adaptation: Give students fewer constraints (perhaps only four instead of the ten ingredients listed in Chapter 5, pp.100–101), less characters to manage and more lesson time to devise. Another idea could be to provide the students with some details (e.g. context, a brief outline of story) which can serve as a springboard for them to use and to prevent them from being overwhelmed by choice, thus scaffolding their learning.

Stardust Excerpt {M, S}:

In small groups, students select an excerpt of text from *Stardust* approved by the teacher. They must update the excerpt with *lazzi* and *burle* to suit the current social and political climate. They are to rehearse to the level of a polished performance in order to persuade their teachers to allow a production of *Stardust* at their school.

{M} adaptation: Students choose shorter scripts so that performance time is shorter.

Choose your own Adventure {S}:

See Making and Shaping section (above) for further details. Students polish and present their devised performance using technology.

Reflection and Analysis of Dramatic Forms—Assessment Possibilities

The following assessment activities are graded for their suitability at various levels of education.

Fantastical Circus Experience Response {LP}:

Students could be asked to draw, paint or construct a diorama of their favourite moment during the Circus experience. It could be a moment they were involved in or a moment they observed. If they are able to write, they could perhaps title this art work or have a teacher write it for them. It is important for the teacher to draw out of students *why* this was their favourite moment.

Report on Commedia {P}:

Students could present a report on one of the short scenarios they observed and explain why it was modern Commedia. Conversely, students could write an article for the school newsletter describing one of the scenarios and again explaining why it was modern Commedia.

Website Review {M}:

The 'Commedia Oz Theatre Troupe' wants to make a website about Commedia in contemporary Australia and needs some reviews of other Commedia websites to gather ideas and make links with existing information. Students choose one Commedia character and report on three existing Commedia websites. They are to compare and contrast information found on the character situations, roles and relationships, and evaluate which website had the best information. They must choose which website/s could be linked to the Commedia Oz website and why.

Live Performance Response {S}:

Take students to the theatre to see a performance that contains a number of Commedia elements (e.g. Shakespeare, farce or physical theatre) and have them prove why it is *not* technically Commedia. Give students a number of elements of Drama to guide the discussion—contrast, timing, mood, etc.

Essay {S}:

Jules Tasca (1992): '[Commedia characters] never become extinct, and will only die when the last man on the planet expires. Their host is humanity. They are as much life as breath and heartbeats.'

Discuss the relevance of Commedia in modern Australian society. In their answers, students are to refer to the history of the genre and the roles and relationships between two stock characters and the audience.

Actor's Journal {M, S}:

Teachers can set questions for actor-students asking them to detail their experiences during the unit and depict the evolution of their Commedia skills. For ideas for questions, see Response Questions throughout this book.

Director's Journal {S}:

Teachers can set questions for director-students asking them to analyse their experiences during the unit (linked to the Directing task in the Making and Shaping section earlier in this Chapter). See director's questions below for inspiration:

1. Has there always been a place for directors in theatre? When? Where?
2. How important is a director to a theatre project or performance? Why?
3. Can actors successfully direct themselves? Give examples from the fields of film, television and theatre.
4. How important is training as a part of a rehearsal process?
5. If training is important, what kind of training should be implemented?
6. What are the biggest problems that actors face during rehearsals and leading up to performance? How can they be solved?

7. Can rehearsals prepare an actor for an audience? If yes, what techniques can assist actors to be ready for an audience?

Commedia Oz {S}:

Ask students to read Steven's introduction to *Stardust* and Nicky's excerpts from her Actor's Journal found throughout this book, as well as the interview with Jacques Lecoq (Chapter 6). How is Commedia created, rehearsed and performed in Australia today?

Post-performance Essay {S}:

After their Commedia stage experience, students answer the following question:

> Author Justin Cartwright in his novel, *Half in Love*, said, 'The creative act is an appalling thing, the offering of one's self to scrutiny'. Do you think this is true for acting? In what ways?

In their answer, students could refer to roles and relationships and focus.

GLOSSARY OF TERMS

Commedia

Arlecchino	servant character
Braggart	someone who boasts, a term usually associated with Il Capitano
Brighella	thug for hire—servant character
burle (pl)/ *burla* (sing)	verbal comedy—extended witty banter and wordplay, often advancing the plot
canovacci (pl)/ *canovaccio* (sing)	list of Commedia scenes
Columbina	unmasked servant character—often Arlecchino's girlfriend
Commedia dell'arte	(pronounced 'com-med-ee-ya dell art-ay') Comedy of Professional Artists or Skilled Comedy (in the tradition of craft guilds such as goldsmiths, stonemasons); improvised Italian comedy with half masks popular from approx. 1550–1700
countermask	atypical attributes of characters (e.g. kindness in the cruel Brighella)
dolt	idiot
grummelot	term created by French Commedia actors to describe gibberish or nonsense languages which could be used to convey the sense of a speech without having to use an actual language
Il Capitano	stupid braggart foreigner with little experience in real military matters
Il Dottore	'educated' master character—old man
improvisation	inventive ad-libbing, winging it
inamorata	female lover, unmasked, often called Isabella or Dorabella
inamorato	male lover, unmasked, often called Flavio or Lelio

innuendo	much of Commedia uses insinuation, or suggestion, without actually spelling out the humour; often used in sexual jokes (e.g. Columbina flatters Capitano: 'My goodness, what a large sword you've got!')
Isabella	common name of inamorata (female lover)—an unmasked character (sometimes called Dorabella or other romantic name)
lazzi (pl.)/ *lazzo* (sing.)	physical comedy and tricks (e.g. slipping on a banana skin or doing a back flip to avoid getting hit)
Lelio	common name of inamorato (male lover)—an unmasked character (sometimes called Flavio or other romantic name)
misanthrope	person who despises humankind (e.g. Pantalone)
mill and seethe	students move purposefully throughout the Drama space, listening for instructions from the workshop leader
miser	stingy with money (e.g. Pantalone)
Pantalone	miserly master character—old man
phallic	resembling phallus or penis
physicality	slapstick, mime and gesture—physical language of Commedia
Pulcinella	servant character—sometimes shy and birdlike, sometimes cruel
satire	send-up or spoof
scenario	summary or outline of the plot in written form
slapstick	stick for hitting in comedy; traditionally two planks of wood separated by a handle that makes a loud 'slap'—the term has evolved into referring to physical tricks
Tartaglia	stutterer—servant or master character
tippi fissi	stock characters
Zanni	generic servant character
zibaldone	in traditional Commedia, a book passed down from generation to generation filled with monologues, poems, etc.

Improvisation

offer	improviser 'A' initiates a scene, an action or dialogue (e.g. 'Excuse me, do you have the time?')
accept	improviser 'B' goes with the offer and accepts it (e.g. 'Yes, it's midnight')

block	if 'B' answers 'No', they block the offer and the scene can stop in its tracks
risk	'B' can advance the scene by taking a risk (e.g. 'Yes. But I'm not giving it to you. I hate you. I've always hated you.') The improviser has taken a risk with the scene by increasing the stakes (suggesting the characters have a history). This response might quickly get the scene cooking because of the risk taken.
yield	give way to the risk. (If upon hearing they are hated, 'A' may respond with, 'I don't know you'—a potential block. Another way might be to say, 'Why do you hate me? What have I ever done to you?')
advance	'B' advances the story by providing new information or jumping to a new episode or event with a fresh offer (e.g. 'You're my father. You abandoned me and Mum when I was a baby. I know you from photographs.')
endow	'B' gives qualities to an object or role ('Mum tells me you were a terrible father and husband. You went out one night for a bottle of milk and never came back. Here, I have a photograph of you.' 'B' shows a picture in their wallet.)
extend	provide more of the story (e.g. the father may continue or extend the scene by going into detail about why he abandoned the mum and child; he can tell of sailing overseas to find a fortune to send back to them and being shipwrecked for years and so on)
transition	at a certain point the scene may need a transition to a new location or a shift in emotion and/or mood. A good improviser knows when this moment has arrived. It might be as simple as the father saying, 'I'm dying of cancer. My one wish was to see your mother and you before I die. Please take me to her.'
protect	good improvisers are constantly protecting their fellow improvisers. If an improviser is stuck for ideas in the scene, or floundering for words, the other improviser/s will help them out within the context of their characters and the scene. If all actors or improvisers are protecting their fellow performers, even things that go wrong become creative possibilities.

status	one's place in society (e.g. a king is high status, a servant is low status)—Drama (comedy and tragedy) is heavily driven by the status of characters and changes in status.
status reversal	when someone who is traditionally high status becomes low status and vice versa. The downtrodden (low status) common character finally stands up against the (high status) crook or bully. Sometimes, though, battles to be the lowest status can be engaging and often comic.

'RESAUCES' and REFERENCES

BOOKS AND JOURNALS

Appel, Libby 1982, *Mask Characterization: An Acting Process*, Southern Illinois University Press, Carbondale.

Callery, Dymphna 2001, *Through the Body: A Practical Guide to Physical Theatre*, Nick Hern Books, London.

Cartwright, Justin 2001, *Half in Love*, Hodder Headline, Sydney.

Crawford, Jerry L. 1995, *Acting in Person and in Style*, 5th edn, William C Brown, Dubuque.

Ducharte, P. L. 1966, *The Italian Comedy: The Improvisation, Scenarios, Lives*, trans. R.T. Weaver, Dover Publications, New York.

Erenstein, Robert L. 1990, *Commedia dell'Arte and the Comic Spirit*, Actors Theater of Louisville, Louisville.

Fava, Antonio 2007, *The Comic Mask in the Commedia dell'Arte—Actor Training, Improvisation and the Poetics of Survival*, Northwestern University Press, Evanston.

Fo, Dario 1988, *Mistero Buffo*, trans. Ed Emergy,Methuen, London.

Fo, Dario 1991, *Tricks of the Trade*, ed. Stuart Hood, trans. Joe Farrell, Routledge, New York.

Gordon, Mel 1983, *Lazzi: The Comic Routines of Commedia dell'arte*, Performing Arts Journal Publications, New York.

Grantham, Barry 2000, *Playing Commedia: A Training Guide to Commedia Techniques*, Nick Hern Books, London.

Gration, Steven 1991, 'Arts People—Jacques Lecoq' in *Lowdown*, North Adelaide, June, pp. 22–25.

Harwood, Ronald 1984, *All the World's a Stage*, Secker and Warburg, London.

Jarry, Alfred 1961, *Ubu Roi*, trans. Barbara Wright, Gaberbocchus Press, London.

Johnstone, Keith 1981, *Impro: Improvisation and the Theatre*, Methuen, London.

Lawler, Lillian B. 1964, *The Dance of the Ancient Greek Theatre*, University of Iowa Press, Iowa City.

Lecoq, Jacques, Lallias, Jean-Claude & Carasso, Jean-Gabriel 2001, *The Moving Body—Teaching Creative Theatre*, trans. David Bradby, Routledge, New York.

Linklater, Kristin 1976, *Freeing the Natural Voice*, Drama Book Specialists, New York.

Pierse, Lyn 1995, *Theatresports Down Under: A Guide for Coaches and Players*, Improcorp, Kensington, .

Rudlin, John 1994, *Commedia dell'Arte: An Actor's Handbook*, Routeledge, London.

Rudlin, John & Crick, Olly 2001, *Commedia dell'arte: A Handbook for Troupes*, Routeledge, London.

Spolin, Viola 1963, *Improvisation for the Theater: A Handbook of Teaching and Directing Techniques*, Northwestern University Press, Evanston, Illinois.

Tasca, J. 1992, *Commedia dell'arte: Plays for a Modern Audience*, Samuel French, New York.

INTERNET SITES

There are many Commedia-specific internet sites and associated links to other sites. A few are listed below:

www.geocities.com/commedia_dellarte/Characters/characters.html: very good detailed information on characters.

www.delpiano.com/carnival/html/commedia.html: contains some dubious information but is interesting nonetheless for comparison.

http://italian.about.com/library/weekly/aa110800a.htm

www.groups.yahoo.com/group/commediadellarte

FILMS

There are hundreds of films and television programs that contain Commedia influences and resonances. A few sources of inspiration and debate are listed below:

Bullets Over Broadway (US film) 1994, Director Woody Allen. For a twisted love triangle and a gangster-Brighella character.

The Castle (Oz film) 1997, Director Rob Sitch. For contemporary Commedia characters and the theme of bully versus the little person.

The Chaser's War on Everything (Oz TV series), ABC Television. For a look at five zany Aussie guys improvising and stirring up trouble in public places!

Commedia by Fava—The Commedia dell'arte Step by Step (DVD) 2006, Contemporary Arts Media.

Dr Plonk (Oz film) 2007, Director Rolf de Heer. A black-and-white silent film made with a traditional hand-cranked camera, featuring lots of slapstick and *lazzi*. Performed by Magda Szubanski, Adelaide street performer Nigel Lunghi, Paul Blackwell and his dog Reg.

The Great Dictator (US film) 1940, directed by and featuring Charlie Chaplin; *Chaplin* 1992 (US Film), with Robert Downey Jr. portraying Chaplin; and other many other films starring Chaplin (some available on VHS and DVD).

Home Alone 1990, *Home Alone 2: Lost in New York* 1992, *and Home Alone 3* 1997. US film series containing fine examples of *lazzi*.

Kenny (Oz film) 2006, Director Clayton Jacobson. for a contemporary Arlecchino and his quest for love and happiness.

Laurel and Hardy; Abbott and Costello; The Marx Brothers; and The Three Stooges. Any US films and television programs featuring these comic teams.

Les Deux Voyages de Jacques Lecoq (French film) 1999, Paris, La Sept ARTE, On Line Productions, ANRAT, Directors Roy, Jean-Nöel & Carasso, Jean-Gabriel.

Monty Python and the Holy Grail 1975, *The Life of Brian* 1979 and *The Meaning of Life* 1983. UK films featuring the Monty Python team and 'The Ministry of Silly Walks' sketch from their UK TV series *Monty Python's Flying Circus*.

Mr Bean character played by Rowan Atkinson (UK films and TV series).

Much Ado About Nothing (UK film) 1993, Director Kenneth Branagh. Film of Shakespeare play, especially for Michael Keaton's character, Sheriff, and Ben Elton's character, Assistant, for *lazzi*, *burle*, dialects and invisible horses.

Pirates of the Caribbean: The Curse of the Black Pearl 2003, *Pirates of the Caribbean: Dead Man's Chest* 2006 and *Pirates of the Caribbean: At World's End* 2007. US/UK film series, for various Commedia-type characters, romance, fights, *lazzi*, *burle* and social sequences.

Shakespeare in Love (UK/US film) 1998. For Elizabethan period romance and comedy from a similar time to the heyday of Commedia dell'arte. Lots of resonances with The Lovers, the Tartaglia character and physical comedy.

Please see: Chapter 2 (character description section) under 'Modern Day Character Resonances' for more film, television and theatre references related to Commedia dell'arte.

AUSTRALIAN MASK-MAKERS

Peter Donahue (peternov@tpg.com.au) for leather masks.

Darkside Masks www.darksidemasks.com for latex masks.

ILLUSTRATIONS

Benjamin Drake (www.benjamindrake.blogspot.com).

PHOTOGRAPHY

Lucas Dawson www.lucasdawson.com.au.

The mask photographs in Commedia Oz were taken by Lucas Dawson who also photographs major events such as Melbourne Cup Fashions, World Cup Soccer, NRL Finals and the nightclub/celebrity scene. Surf Lucas' website and spot examples of 'dynamic stillness' positions and potential Commedia characters in his photos. Contemporary Commedia continues to draw its sustenance from all kinds of human activities and behaviour.

Trataglia
Illustration by Benjamin Drake

INDEX

Page references in **bold** text indicate an image.